FLYING
MARY
O'CONNOR

FLYING MARY O'CONNOR

B
Oc 5

FLYING MARY O'CONNOR

by Mary O'Connor

+

illustrated with

fifty photographs

RAND McNALLY & COMPANY
New York · Chicago · San Francisco

61-23794

For the stewardesses of tomorrow,
        the girls who will fly the jets

acknowledgments

The author acknowledges with deep appreciation the generosity of United Air Lines Publicity Department in reading and checking the manuscript and in providing so many illustrations from their picture files. All pictures in the book not specifically mentioned below, are United Air Lines photographs. The picture of Miss O'Connor as a "Navy Rockette" is reprinted from *R.N.—a Journal for Nurses*, April, 1945, by permission. It is Copyright, 1945, by The Nightingale Press, Inc., Oradell, N. J. The letter from Herbert Hoover is reprinted with the gracious permission of its writer. The picture of Wendell Willkie and his wife is a United Press International, Inc. picture. The picture of Mary O'Connor and the *Mainliner O'Connor* is reprinted with the permission of the *Chicago Sun-Times*. The pictures of Nellie Jane DeWitt and Sue Dauser are Official Navy Photographs, reprinted with the permission of the Navy Medical Department. The pictures of Mary O'Connor in her youth, and the pictures of the various diplomas and citations are the personal property of the author.

illustrations

foreword

THE big airplane droned its way through the billowing clouds of fog like a great fish lost in a sea of cloudy water. It bucked head winds as it headed toward San Francisco from Seattle on that morning in 1930, and its ten passengers reacted variously. Some consulted their watches, torn between exasperation and uneasiness; some dozed, drugged with boredom; and still others looked out into the smothering grayness, wondering where it ended and when the trip would.

Belatedly, obviously in a hurry, the co-pilot came through with cups of coffee. Yes, they were late getting in; no, there was no need for uneasiness; they were simply slowed up by the fog and head winds. "Sorry, sir, the coffee spilled—hope it won't stain your coat. Aspirin? I'll look, ma'am,—not sure we have any aboard. Yes, we should get in in another hour . . . ."

Seated well aft, Stephen A. Stimpson, Division
Traffic Agent for United Air Lines, stopped drawing
squares and circles on the margin of his folded newspaper and took a notebook from his pocket. Just this
one flight should prove he'd been right all along.
For months he had been agitating for *some* sort of
attendant service aboard all commercial planes.
There should be someone whose duty it was to see
that passengers were made to feel at home in the air,
someone to be in charge of medical supplies for
minor illnesses, someone to serve coffee who knew
how to do it without drenching a passenger now and
then with the scalding brew. But who should this
nebulous someone be? A Filipino boy? No, it was a
thought, but he put it from him, tapping the end of
his pencil against the window.

How about . . .? His pencil stopped tapping. "Got it!" he said aloud and began furiously to
make notes in his book. When the plane put down
in San Francisco, Stephen Stimpson was still writing,
and that evening he sent a long memo to A. G. Kins-
man, Passenger Traffic Manager. Here, in part, is
what he wrote—and it changed the whole design of
commercial flying:

"As a suggestion I was wondering if you had ever
given any serious thought to the subject of young
women as couriers. It strikes me there would be a

great psychological punch to having young women stewardesses or couriers or whatever you want to call them, and I am certain that there are some mighty good ones available. I have in mind a couple of graduate nurses who would make exceptional stewardesses. Of course, it would be distinctly understood that there would be no reference made to their hospital training or nursing experience, but it would be a mighty fine thing to have this available, sub rosa, if necessary either for air sickness or perhaps something else.

"Imagine the psychology of having young women as regular members of the crew. Imagine the national publicity we would get from it, and the tremendous effect it would have on the traveling public. Also, imagine the value they would be to us in the neater and nicer method of serving food and looking out for the passengers' welfare, but also in an emergency."

There was much more; it was a long, earnest memorandum and it had quick repercussions.

Ellen Church, a young nurse in San Francisco who loved flying, had been wondering whether in some way she could combine the careers of flying and nursing, and when she heard that United Air Lines was seriously considering hiring graduate

Ellen Church, the world's first stewardess, third from left, with the seven nurses she hired

nurses to act as stewardesses aboard its planes, she applied for the position. She was hired, and became the first air stewardess in the world. She hired seven other registered nurses to try out the experiment.

"It's just a trial balloon," the young pioneer told her recruits. "These jobs may not be permanent. They may last only a few weeks."

Those plucky girls went about their duties quietly, efficiently, eager to prove that Stephen Stimpson knew what he was talking about when he convinced United Air Lines how wise and foresighted it was to put stewardesses aboard their planes.

But Ellen's first flight got off to a disconcerting start. Pilots and co-pilots resented the whole stewardess project. Women had invaded far too many fields heretofore dominated exclusively by men,

Ellen Church and Stephen A. Stimpson, thirty years later

they insisted. Now even the air was to be invaded by women. It wasn't right! It didn't make sense! They'd have no part of it!

When Ellen reported to the plane that first morning, she was greeted by the dour-faced pilot. He squared his shoulders. "Look, sister," he said, "the only reason you're on this plane—you or any other girl—is because the company must have gone a little crazy. Get one thing straight, though. You stay in the cabin. Understand? No coming up to the cockpit. We're busy enough as it is, once we're off the ground, and we can't be bothered having girls around, see?"

Ellen nodded cheerfully and went about her business, greeting passengers, distributing gum and newspapers, answering questions, hanging up wraps.

That was a good many years ago, but something happened on a subsequent flight which has become flying history.

Naturally, pilots were changed from one flight to another, but Ellen soon learned that they all shared a glowering antagonism toward stewardesses as crew members. On a day during her first week on duty, when flying from Cheyenne to Salt Lake City, she could not help noticing that one of her passengers was in acute distress. She questioned him several times and after making a simple examination was convinced he was suffering from appendicitis. She went up to the cockpit and asked the pilot to radio ahead for a doctor to meet the plane at Rock Springs, an unscheduled stop on the way. And here she met her first real rebuff.

"Wouldn't you know it!" The pilot addressed the sky without turning. "A guy gets a stomach ache from eating too much lunch and just because there's a stewardess aboard he raises the roof. Tell him to pipe down. We've got mail aboard for Salt Lake City and that's where we're going. Now beat it!"

Little Ellen's chin came up. "You forget," she told the flinty young man at the controls, "that I am a registered nurse and I recognize the symptoms. The man has acute appendicitis and every second counts. Radio for help or I'll not be responsible!"

That put quite another light on the matter. Reluctantly the pilot radioed and the plane put down at Rock Springs where a doctor and an ambulance were waiting. The little nurse's diagnosis was correct. The sick man was rushed to the hospital and an emergency operation was performed which undoubtedly saved his life. The red-faced pilot apologized. The world's first stewardess had shown how important the presence of trained women aboard all airplanes could be.

Quickly the stewardess plan was taken up by other sections of United Air Lines' coast-to-coast and Pacific systems; then other air lines adopted it. The number of stewardesses grew until hundreds of young women were taking a recognized place aboard planes of air lines both in the United States and abroad. Today, thirty years later, there are about ten thousand stewardesses serving in the world's air service. Stephen Stimpson's vision and initiative alone are responsible.

One of the earliest and most winning of the "sky girls," as they were called at first, and certainly the "flyingest" of them all was Mary O'Connor, with more than six million miles to her credit. But let her tell her story.

—THE PUBLISHERS

Mary O'Connor in her youth. Upper left: at 4; lower left: with her sister Marguerite; upper right: at confirmation; lower right: at grade school graduation

chapter 1

WE were an awfully happy, more or less care-free family, we O'Connors, in our big, old-fashioned house on Chicago's northwest side. There were five of us—Mother, Dad, my sister, three years older than I, and our young brother, born when we girls were in our teens. Mother was a born conservative who accepted very little at its face value; Mother had to be shown—and she usually was—before she reached a decision. Dad, on the other hand, had the sunny, trusting nature of a true son of the South of Ireland and the results as far as we children were concerned were obvious: we loved and "minded" Mother; we adored Dad and twisted him around our fingers.

After the primary and intermediate years in the neighborhood parochial school, I attended St. Patrick's Academy for the usual four-year preparatory

course, and then, circumstances dictating that college had better be forgotten, for the time being at
any rate, I looked for my first job and got it with the
Palmolive Company.

The work—clerical—was interesting and the
pay fair. I was promoted, learned to use a comp-
tometer and figured salesmen's commissions. But
isn't it strange that if, deep within you there is an
urge to do some one special thing, all the promotions
in another field, no matter how generous, simply do
not matter? You know what you want, and *that* is
what you are going after. And you know, it is amaz-
ing when you come to think of it, the reasons for
choosing a certain career have a way of dovetailing
along across time until suddenly, pft! there you are
and you know the dovetailing has stopped. You have
arrived and you're going to stay.

Somehow, as long as I can remember I've
wanted to be a nurse, so it was only natural that after
graduation from St. Patrick's, I should give it rather
special thought. However, the job with Palmolive
presented itself so quickly that I took it almost without thinking. But even then, subconsciously I was
looking for a hospital in which to begin my training.
Mother knew what was on my mind and she was not
pleased. A nurse? Now why a nurse? Certainly there
must be pleasanter vocations. Why a nurse whose

work necessarily involved so much that was ugly and sordid and just plain unpleasant? Mother was really in quite a state. Dad didn't exactly wink at me, but his little boy grin implied, "What are we waiting for? If it's a nurse you're wanting to be, darlin', well then, go ahead, and be the very best nurse you know how to be."

Both Mother and Dad knew I had a will of my own once my mind was made up, so no more was said about nursing, and I started out making the rounds. I cannot tell you how many hospitals I visited, and as I walked away from each one I knew the ugly, sinking feeling that comes with discouragement. So by trial and error, by street car and elevated train, I finally arrived at the St. Francis Hospital Nurses' Home in Evanston, Illinois. It was a golden September day in 1929 and right there is where I like to think the dovetailing settled down to business. Here at last was a beginning after many false starts. I looked up at St. Francis smiling benevolently down at me from an arched doorway and prayed I'd be worthy of the opportunity to learn, to serve.

It was the beginning of four of the happiest years I had known. I found I loved every single thing about my chosen field. Where was the drudgery, the filth Mother and many of my friends had warned me about? The daily routine of trays, bedpans, dressings, hypos—these were all simply part of the whole challenge to my youthful strength and enthusiasm. When graduation day came and my cap was pinned in place, I was still the starry-eyed Florence Nightingale with her mind firmly fixed on a career in nursing.

Now I was an R.N., a registered nurse. It did not seem possible that I, Mary O'Connor, should be sailing forth into a tormented world to help heal its ills. Nothing could stop me now, I was sure. But nevertheless, something did . . . for a time at least.

The United States was wallowing in the trough of the blackest financial depression the country ever had known. Banks were closing, jobs gradually were becoming non-existent; there were apple sellers on every corner. And who, just *who* could afford a private nurse? To be sure, there were still the comparatively rich minority and the hospitals did occasionally call for a private nurse. By and large, however, if you were desperately sick you went to the hospital and for a few days you did have the care of an R.N.; otherwise, you remained at home and the family looked after you. No calls came from the Nurses' Registry, though undoubtedly all over the country graduate nurses, their bags packed, sat beside their home telephones, waiting. I was among them. Just at first the waiting was not too trying. You told yourself a little bleakly that it gave you time to get well rested. What, after all, was to be gained by rushing from case to case? Only—what case? Before long rent had to be paid (in a fine glow of independence I was living in a rented room not far from the hospital), and food and clothing had to be managed, too.

And just here the dovetailing speed became accelerated. One day when the telephone hadn't rung even by mistake, a friend dropped in. As she was leaving, "Look," she said, "have you ever thought of flying—you know, being a stewardess?"

"Me? A stewardess? Fly? Heavens, no! I don't even know anyone who's been up in a plane. Why did you ask?" What an idiotic notion, I thought.

My friend shrugged as she opened the door. "Honestly I don't know, except that I heard United Air Lines was hiring graduate nurses as stewardesses. Send for one of their application forms anyway. What can you lose?"

It made sense. What could I lose? And meanwhile a call might come from the Registry. However, it didn't and the application form did. I wish I could describe the funny little upsurge of something—call it prescience if you want to—that swept over me as I studied that official looking application form. It was a feeling of excitement and delight and dismay all rolled into one. *This* was not what I had planned to do! I was a nurse and very proud to be one. Certainly I wasn't going to throw away those four wonderful years of training to become a stewardess—not me! Yet somewhere in my subconscious a little voice said, "Yes, but Mary, here's a chance to be *both!*"

I filled out the form and mailed it, still uncertain, almost hoping I never would have an answer. However, I did, and quickly. Those were the days of the simple, unembroidered approach, and I was told to come to the Chicago office of United Air Lines for an interview. As I recall, it was brief and pleasant. I was interviewed by the Manager of pilots and stewardesses, a Mr. E. P. Lott, and his questions were rather general: Why did I want to be a stewardess? What had some of my nursing experiences been? Was my general health good? And then, like an unexpected bolt of lightning, was there any reason why I couldn't fly to Kansas City the next day for a physical examination! Mother, when I told her, looked dubious. Dad simply said, "You're the doctor, Mary."

Some things you just never forget, and to the end of my days I shall remember my short walk across the strip from the hangar the next morning to the waiting plane. Mary O'Connor, I kept thinking, you're mad as a March hare to be doing this! You've never been on a plane in your life or even thought you wanted to be, yet here you've taken a job as

Ford tri-motor plane, seating ten

stewardess. What's come over you? Nervously I climbed aboard the little tri-motor Ford plane seating ten and shakily fastened my seat belt.

Anyone who has flown recalls certain sensations of his (or her) first flight. There was the almost unbearable, frightening excitement that caught you by the throat when the engines roared into action, the propellers began to whir, and your plane taxied out on the runway. There it stood while its engines and propellers gathered speed and the entire plane vibrated with the mounting force of their straining power. Any moment you felt it must fly to pieces. Instead, slowly it began to roll forward, then faster, faster, gathering speed until, with a soft little bound it rose, the ground dropped away, and you were airborne.

My own weird sensation—leave it to an Irish redhead—was that we were standing still in the sky and the earth was playing us tricks, was leaving us, dropping into some secret pit of its own and presently would be seen no more! Then when we tilted a bit, straightened out and headed west, the truth blazed at me with a terrific shock: I was flying! Only to me, since my aeronautical vocabulary was still a babe, it registered as "going up," and from that moment of "going up," soaring up and away from the earth, I knew that here was where I belonged. The dovetailing events had faithfully played their parts; they had brought me here and here I would stay. The sky was my home, my love. I knew I would give to it my very best, my nursing ability should it be needed, but first of all my whole devotion in whatever form it might be required. I found that I loved flying. I shall always love flying. I never have known one split second of fear in the air though I have flown through some foul weather and at times under trying conditions. Compared with all other modes of travel, flying has most of the advantages.

On that first flight of mine to Kansas City we averaged a hundred and ten miles an hour—the speed of light, it seemed to me—and though I fairly ached to go up and have a cockpit view of the sky and the ground below, I remembered a briefing I'd had in Chicago, which had included the advice to "stay out of the cockpit," and put the temptation from me.

In Kansas City I had my physical examination, and was told I was a very healthy specimen, but to watch my weight. Then, back in Chicago, I signed various necessary papers and had my uniform fitted. Looking back I can still see that earnest little tailor! His shop or office was right on the field and he made the pilots' uniforms with a real flair. But when it came to fitting women, the results left a lot to be desired. Those first uniforms seemed to bulge—or we did—in all the wrong places.

I returned to Kansas City in my stiff new uniform, feeling just a little cocky perhaps, to get my instructions, and tried with no spectacular success to impress the co-pilots, who were to be responsible for my training, with the fact that I was a human being of at least average intelligence. It seems almost incredible today, but in those first days of stewardess service, pilots really held a very dim view of having their hitherto all-male realm in the sky invaded by women. They just couldn't take it.

My Kansas City lads eyed my determined, hopeful grin with an air of utter boredom. Today if they had been faced with some similiar situation they undoubtedly would have suggested that I get lost. But the expression was unknown then, so they only glared, and in my heart I couldn't blame them. You see, it was their duty to give me my training in their *free time* and the whole idea wore their patience thin. In those days there actually was not much formal training for a stewardess, since no one, from the highest officials down, could be sure what should be included in her duties. In the beginning she just made herself useful in the cabin wherever she might be needed. She greeted passengers when they arrived; she took their tickets, disposed of their wraps, gave them gum and the latest edition of the daily paper, saw them comfortably seated and, before takeoff, reminded them to fasten their seat belts. At meal time she passed the little trays of sandwiches and coffee and later collected the trays. That was about all.

I remained in Kansas City for two weeks and during that time had about one hour of instruction. As the days passed I fought a growing sense of panic and frustration. I wanted my job to begin. Instead, I spent my time window shopping, going to the movies, reading, and finally in desperation counting the sprawling leaves on the wallpaper design in my hotel room! Whenever possible I cornered one of the pilots and plied him with questions, listening avidly to any answers he would bother to give me, and at last the great day arrived. I was to fly aboard the nine o'clock flight from Kansas City to Dallas the next morning! I was awake most of the night, my alarm set for four, but even before it went off I was up and pulling on my shower cap.

Flipping the pages of a United circular, printed in 1933, I find that our uniform was described as "a dapper, double-breasted green uniform (coat and skirt), a man's gray shirt with a starched collar, green string tie, and jaunty green tam." Well, contemplated nearly three decades later, neither "dapper" nor "jaunty" seems quite the right adjective, for there is no denying that double-breasted jackets, at least those we wore, did bunch around the middle and the "jaunty" tams were like nothing so much as dust caps, ruffled and bulging. Nor were the capes mentioned. Ah, those whirling, entangling capes! However, at the time I felt frightfully trim and well gotten up when, still hours ahead of time, I arrived at the airport.

Would I remember all I had tried to assimilate during the one hour of training? Would I be able to serve coffee without spilling it if the flight were rough? Did my slip show? Was my tie on straight? By flight time my hands were clammy with nervousness and I sent up a wild petition that I'd be spared the humiliation of being airsick—I, the perfect stewardess!

The pilot and co-pilot came aboard and greeted me with friendly nonchalance as they went up to the cockpit. The pilot looked at his watch. "Where's the crowd?" he asked, grinning.

The uniform of the first "sky girls," 1930, with
the flowing cape that was designed to ward off
wind blast from the propellers

Well, yes, where was it? Not a single passenger came aboard for that maiden voyage of mine! However, it couldn't be helped. My hands grew warmer and my stomach steadier and after we were airborne I served the crew breakfast without any mishaps and even won a "Nice going, Miss O'Connor!"

The return trip was more interesting. I had four passengers, one of them Buddy Rogers, Mary Pickford's husband, and since that flight no one has ever been able to tell me women alone are impressed by celebrities. Mr. Rogers asked to borrow my comb and he'd no sooner returned it to me than one of the three men passengers offered to buy it! I gave it to him. That was in May 1933.

Those first few weeks settled me into the routine of flying. Eddie Stewart, a co-pilot, taught me a lot about the finer points of being a stewardess: how always to be prepared for a lurch when carrying a tray or even a glass of water; how to keep smiling no matter what the circumstances. And Charlie Peoples, a pilot, part Indian, gave me some of the soundest advice on deportment that any green young stewardess ever received. Charlie was a remarkable man, a really brilliant pilot. He went to South America and I've often wondered what became of him.

It was on June 1, 1933 that the first *Boeing 247* streamlined ten-passenger planes were put into serv-

The Boeing 247, recognized as the immediate ancestor of today's airliners, put into service in June 1933

ice between Chicago and New York, a five-hour flight, and I was one of the four stewardesses assigned to those flights.

Compared with today's huge, sleek *Mainliners*, they were small and cramped, but to us who had graduated from the little *tri-motor Fords*, they seemed colossal. The day of two stewardesses to a plane was still in the future, and frankly, I don't know how two of us could have managed without breaking some bones. The planes seated only ten passengers and as there were two wing struts across the aisle, and the aisle narrow, every trip the stewardess made up or down it, especially if there was turbulence, became something of an obstacle race. Think if there had been two of us!

Business men were just beginning to appreciate the wonderful convenience of air travel and before long there were regular commuters flying with us several times a week. In fact, in those free-handed, unconventional days when any of our "regulars" failed to put in an appearance on their regular day, we thought nothing of contacting the Traffic Department and having them see whether all was well. On the other hand, if by any chance one of our commuters was delayed in getting to the airport, he simply telephoned and we waited for him.

Those were the apprenticeship days when we were all a little crude, all eager to attain something remotely akin to the perfection we are approaching today. Though I've flown more than six million miles and in some of the most luxurious of our modern planes, there is still a nostalgic tug at my heartstrings for the early learn-as-you-fly days of 1933.

And speaking of learning, the meals we served back yonder never by any stretch of the imagination could have insinuated themselves under the heading "Chef's Special for Today." At first there were the sandwiches-and-coffee refreshers; then, later, came identical lunch and dinner menus consisting of cold fried chicken, potato chips, roll, dessert, and coffee. The result was that anyone traveling from California to New York was likely to face the same combination three times en route. One waggish Californian observed quietly over his third chicken-potato chip meal that he thought if we opened a window he could fly the rest of the way! Breakfast consisted of a sweet roll and coffee, and for in-between snacks there were cookies. Considering the struts we negotiated with our meager offerings, however, and the amount of coffee that frequently went cascading across the trays, I wonder what we would have done with the feasts that are served today. We were quite dexterous, a pretty sure-footed lot, though, and I'm sure we would have made out somehow.

But on that very first trip from Chicago to New York aboard the *Boeing 247* I made the serious mistake of thinking I knew more than I actually did and the results might have been serious. Before we left Chicago I cornered the Mate—we call them First Officers today—and from him I got the necessary flight information, arrival times, etc. Unfortunately that nice cooperative boy was as ignorant as I! In completely good faith he told me Cleveland would be our first stop.

At that time the Public Address System had not been installed on planes, so how was I to know when we came in for our first landing that it was *not* Cleveland? I had eight passengers—four for Cleveland and four for Newark. I helped the four Cleveland-bound passengers on with their overcoats, said good-by, and watched them walk away toward the baggage shed to claim their bags. A few minutes passed and then over the Public Address System in the airport building came the announcement of the flight . . . "Four passengers for Cleveland, four for Newark." I couldn't believe I was hearing right.

"Isn't *this* Cleveland?" I shouted in the worst possible stewardess manner to the Mate.

"Gosh, no," my well-meaning friend yelled as he raced by me, down the steps and across the strip. "Let me find those guys in the baggage shed! *It's Toledo!*"

He collected his "guys" and amid a lot of laughter and good-natured ribbing directed at the red-faced stewardess, we were off for Cleveland. That sort of thing could not happen today, not only because the Public Address System aboard the plane would make it impossible, but because today's highly specialized training of stewardesses would have had me letter perfect in every detail of the flight before I set foot aboard the plane. But those were the early days of commercial flying and we still had a good many lessons to learn.

With lessons learned that hard way, there were some awfully heartwarming experiences, too. I shall never forget my first Christmas aloft. The day was depressing when we left Cheyenne, a heavy drizzle and fog pursued us all the way to Omaha; it was the afternoon of Christmas Eve and somehow, in spite of being homesick myself, knowing well all the fun that was in full swing at home, I kept wondering about the passengers. What were they doing away from home on Christmas Eve? Certainly nothing but the most pressing emergency could have brought them aboard. Some might reach Chicago in time for a family celebration, it was true, but in such weather suppose we just couldn't make Chicago? And that was precisely what happened.

We were notified that the Chicago airport was closed in by fog, no planes arriving or departing! The passengers took the news very well, but you could not fail to see how concerned they were. And their concern attached itself like glue to me. We put them aboard an east-bound train at Omaha, hoping to pick them up later at Des Moines or Iowa City, and I went to the hotel. I'm not as a rule given to crying into my soup, but this was one time when it seemed to me I just could not bear the clammy loneliness of that hotel room, looking out into fog so thick that it wiped out even the buildings across the street.

I had just about settled down to a maudlin self-pitying bout of sniveling when the telephone rang. To my amazement it was the pilot of our plane. I never had flown with him before; in fact we were practically strangers, and certainly I did not know that Omaha was his home. Now here he was, his wife chiming in, inviting me to share their Christmas Eve celebration. I was a stranger, yet as I walked into that lovely home I knew all the warmth and sincere hospitality of old friends.

What an evening it was! A delicious dinner; three adorable children explaining carefully that though the tree was always trimmed and ready for Christmas Eve by Mummie and Daddy (if he was home), Santa didn't come until just before dawn the next morning; carols around the piano with "Mummie" playing the accompaniment; and finally the drive back to the hotel with the whole dear family packed into the car to see that I had no chance to lose the spirit of the evening by being alone on a bus or trolley. It was a Christmas Eve I shall always remember. Indeed how could I possibly forget it with those Good Samaritans now some of the closest friends I have? What an unexpectedly lovely Christmas gift!

Nor was that quite all. Early the following morning the telephone rang again. I wondered whether the weather had improved and we were to resume the flight. However, the voice at the other end was that of the Passenger Agent. He was at the airport, and knowing we were still fog-bound and that I would like to attend an early morning church service, he was calling to say he would pick me up in time to make the six o'clock Mass. Another friendly gesture far from home. Christmas ended happily, to the best of my knowledge, for every one of our passengers who was picked up finally at Iowa City and flown without further incident to Chicago. No Christmas passes that I do not hear from one or two of the passengers who shared that long-ago Christmas flight.

A good many years have passed since then. Today, with flights so much shorter in time covered, a Christmas Eve flight is by no means the unaccountable thing it was back in the thirties. Many a passenger flies home on Christmas Eve and flies back on Christmas night in order to be at business the following day, and it is for these travelers that the cabins of the *Mainliners* are given their holiday dress. Holly and pine are festooned by experts to transform the cabins into sweet-smelling bowers; eggnog is passed to cheer the traveler on his way, and lunch (or dinner) is the festive meal complete with turkey and "fixins." Women passengers receive Christmas corsages and the men have boutonnieres tucked into their lapels. Aloft we are very gay, very Christmas-minded, indeed.

chapter 2

CHANGES came slowly but with paradoxical swiftness, considering all that was involved. The first little tri-motor planes made the coast-to-coast flight in about thirty-three and a half hours, their cruising speed running approximately a hundred and fifteen miles an hour. They carried ten to fourteen passengers; they were noisy, badly ventilated, and the pilots used a simple road map for their navigation guide.

Though the *Boeing 247* carried no greater number of passengers, it was an all-metal, streamlined plane traveling at a hundred and eighty miles an hour and the coast-to-coast flight time was reduced to twenty-seven hours.

In 1936 the *DC 3* twin-engine plane had arrived, carrying twenty-one passengers. Now hot meals were served, the equipment was both more

DC 3, 1936, carrying twenty-one passengers

efficient and more elaborate, and flying time to the coast had dropped again—now to twenty-two hours. By 1940 when World War II crashed over the nation, the *DC 4* was in the air, carrying forty-four passengers. It seemed, then, to be the last word in flying comfort.

In 1936 our first lumpy green uniforms and ugly dust-cap tams were replaced by a light-gray double-breasted uniform worn with a gray blouse and a hat shaped something like a pecan shell, with gray and blue streamers at the side. A blue Ascot tie completed the outfit and it was remarkable how becoming the whole thing was to practically everyone. The summer uniform of 1937 was a white one-piece dress with a dark blue sweater-type jacket, and a white hat trimmed in blue. That winter the gray blouse was replaced by one of dark blue, but the coat chosen for us was not a favorite. It was a voluminous thing of heavy gray worsted that looked like nothing so much as a tent. The girls who became brides that year were all most enthusiastic in their praise of those tent-like coats when used for maternity wear! It was in 1940 with the arrival of the *DC 4* that we graduated to a really smart two-piece navy blue suit with a handsome coat to match, chic blue hat, white open-mesh blouse, and dark blue, Cuban-heeled pumps. Scarves and gloves were white—and spotless always.

But let's go back to 1936 and our handsome new *DC 3's*. They really were beautiful planes and we had reached a new high mark in luxurious travel. Some were converted to fourteen-passenger de luxe models with large, richly upholstered wing chairs; meals in elaborate courses served on tables on Haviland china with sterling silver and the finest damask.

DC 4, 1940, carrying forty-four passengers

Top: Mary O'Connor (extreme left) and others in the 1937 "tent-like" winter coat; Left: Mary O'Connor and colleagues in the 1939 summer uniform; Facing page: Graduation ceremony, showing 1940 uniform. D. F. Magarrell, now United's senior vice president transportation services, is pinning on the last pair of wings.

Others were converted into sleeper planes, to be known as *DST* planes. These contained seven compartments: one, well forward, was a sort of lounge and the remaining six could be transformed into berths, an upper and a lower in each group.

I was on hand for the maiden flight of the first sleeper plane. I was wildly enthusiastic and a little jittery about the new routine and more than a little nervous about making up the first berth. It was an upper and had been reserved, I was told, by a man who had asked specifically to have it ready when he arrived as he wanted to go to sleep if possible before we were airborne.

So, eager to have everything perfect, I made up that one berth long before flight time—and waited. When my passenger arrived I found he was a portly, florid, chuffy old gentleman with a bristling white mustache and piercing, cold blue eyes, a man accustomed to giving orders and having them obeyed.

He piled into his berth immediately and drew the curtains, and I went about my duties, greeting passengers, assigning them to their seats, etc. Suddenly I remembered that I had neglected to tell him to fasten his seat belt so that I would not have to disturb him if he should have gone to sleep before we took off.

I rattled his curtains, explained about the belt, and heard his "Thank you very much."

When we were airborne, to my embarrassment I recalled that I should have mentioned the air vent in his berth which he might not know how to regulate. So once more I waggled the curtain, again apologized and explained, and again heard a muffled "Thank you very much." Then I served a light supper to those who wanted it, made up another berth or two, and suddenly remembered that I hadn't told my old gentleman what time he must get up in order to make a nice appearance when he arrived in Chicago early in the morning!

No one will ever know how hard it was to summon up my courage to have another go at those curtains. I gave them a quick jerk and this time with electric results. The curtains flew apart and, scarlet with fury, the old gentleman glared down at me.

"Young woman," he shouted, "this is outrageous! Seat belts, air vents, the rising bell, indeed! Thunderation and charge! Whether I retire from the Army or simply for the night, I *retire!* (He pronounced it 'retiah.') Now go away and let me alone!"

That was decades ago, but I can still feel the wave of suffocating embarrassment that swept over me. I can still see the smiles of the other passengers. It was a bad moment. My initiation into the sleeper service taught me how much more important a calm, unhurried approach to any job is than too much unorganized enthusiasm.

I shall always feel that time spent at night aboard an air liner sleeping in a berth is a great waste unless one is ill or completely exhausted. It seems such a pity to miss any of the beauties of night flying. The twinkling lights of cities far below have a fairy-tale quality, and just to look about at the heavens stretched on all sides with the stars so close that you feel you can reach out and gather them in by the handful, this is an experience one never forgets. On the reverse side of the picture, in stormy weather when rain beats against the windows and your sturdy plane bucks a little like a gallant ocean liner in a gale, there is an indescribable coziness, an at-home-ness about the snug, friendly cabin that is wonderful. Night flying to the air-minded is unique in travel pleasure.

I recall a dear old lady on one of my night flights from Chicago to New York who sat with her face pressed to the window, apparently fascinated by the darkness outside. It was rather an overcast night so there was little to be seen. When the pilot came through the cabin on a routine checking trip, she hailed him. She had noticed the red port and green starboard lights on the wings and asked him what they were. He explained that they were navigation lights, and went on his way, and the old lady, after thanking him, resumed her vigil. When we reached New York that dear little soul told me to be sure to thank the pilots for such a beautiful trip and to tell them how clever she thought they were to be able to keep so perfectly in the lane between the two navigation lights all the way over! She was being welcomed by her family and I was busy with other matters before I fully realized what she had said.

Somehow she had decided that those two lights were blazed across the sky to make a path for our plane. That they were an integral part of the plane itself had not dawned upon her.

My little old lady's pleasure in her trip has been reflected by women everywhere traveling by air since then. True, I knew a lot of them were flying, but not long ago I went over some of the records in my office and even I, the world's leading optimist, could scarcely believe what I read. Would you believe that recent figures show that sixty-one percent of United Air Lines' air tourist passengers and more than thirty percent of the standard fare passengers are women? The women, too, may be responsible for the vast improvement in the meals served aboard planes today, for no woman with a well-equipped kitchen at home would have put up with the cold chicken and potato chip feasts the pioneer passengers, mostly men, faced in the early days.

In 1936 just about the time the *DC 3* was launched, United Air Lines retained D. F. Magarrell, (see picture, page 41) a specialist in food management. He organized a dining service department and in December 1936 he established the world's first flight kitchen in Oakland, California. All sorts of new culinary techniques were perfected under him; the company's engineers devised containers and carriers to keep foods and beverages at desired temperatures, and the era of fine fare for air travelers had dawned.

Nowadays, menus are submitted five weeks in advance to the superintendent of dining service for correlation so that coast-to-coast travelers will not be served the same meal twice in succession. As a matter of fact, they will not encounter a repetition in a week.

Twenty or thirty minutes before a plane leaves the ground, hot food boxes are loaded on carts which have outlets for plug-in to portable generators on the airport ramp while awaiting transfer to the galley of the plane. The boxes of hot and cold foods fit snugly into sections of the galley. Hot food boxes and liquid containers plug into the *Mainliner's* twenty-eight-volt electric system. Trays of salads, desserts, and other cold foods are stacked in boxes that have dry ice as a refrigerant.

The cold fried chicken saga of 1933 is mercifully a thing of the past and United's chefs today turn out more than one thousand menus each year. Flight kitchens—fifteen of them stretched across our 14,000-mile system—are manned by chefs who learned their art in the finest European restaurants and hotels. From Chicago come the choicest cuts of prime beef, from Boston the finest lobster, and

World's first flight kitchen, Oakland, Calif., December 1936

when we fly out of Denver we always have a galley stuffed with the most delicate mountain trout.

The chefs have always been awfully generous about distributing bulletins giving recipes of the most popular dishes and all sorts of cooking hints. And all these heavenly recipes are ours, the stewardesses, for the asking. With such a variety of excitement and so much delicious food into the bargain, how could you possibly help being fond of your job as a stewardess?

Improvements continue in the service rendered aboard the beautiful planes and today when several of us who began our careers "back when" get together we never fail to marvel at the wonders being done to make flying the glorious experience it is. And let's admit it, we do go into gales over some of the zany incidents, the ridiculous situations that often confronted us during the thirties and forties. Our grandmothers would have called them "character building" and who shall say, perhaps they were.

With the coming of the *DC 4*, two stewardesses instead of only one were aboard every plane and at first it seemed strange to those of us who had had a plane to ourselves. However, by the end of a week we wondered how we ever had managed alone. I remember we had a sort of game between us which I declare I think must have originated the "What's My Line?" program on TV and radio. I rather suspect the game continues among stewardesses today, the game of trying to guess the passengers' occupations or professions as they come aboard. One such guess backfired on me with a resounding bang that still makes me want to crawl for cover whenever I think of it.

One day a well-dressed, distinguished looking

man boarded our plane at Chicago bound for New York. Just one look was enough for me to spot him as a doctor, probably a great specialist, I decided. The very way he smoothed his shining gray hair as he handed me his hat, the fact that he wore a handsome wafer-thin watch on a chain across his waistcoat instead of the inevitable wristwatch, all this spelled D-o-c-t-o-r. And sure enough, when I picked up his ticket, there it was! His name was Doctor Alex Smith. Because travel was light that day and I really had time on my hands, I chatted with "Doctor" Smith off and on throughout the flight.

He told me he had been chief surgeon in one of San Francisco's leading hospitals, but that a New York hospital had begged him to replace its chief of staff who was retiring. Reluctantly, since the offer was one he really couldn't afford to decline, he was on his way there now to "at least look over the ground." Ah, but the San Francisco hospital—what a staff! What equipment! The very thought of leaving made him feel a traitor. He turned to the window, his voice a little rough, and I thought I caught a suspicion of tears in his eyes as he looked away. What a dedicated man! What true nobility of soul!

He gave me two notes of introduction: one to a Miss B., the receptionist at the San Francisco hospital; and the other to a Doctor C., on the staff, a bachelor and a young man of the highest integrity. The next time I had a few free hours in San Francisco I must not fail to visit the hospital and meet these two fine young people who would be so glad to show me through.

Well, being Mary O'Connor who never was known to keep a good thing to herself, I couldn't wait until I told my friends about Doctor Alex Smith. In fact, everyone got a little tired of him. A few weeks later when two other United stewardesses and I found ourselves in San Francisco, guess what we chose as our first port of call? Of course, the hospital that Doctor Alex Smith so recently had dignified with his presence. No three nurses ever went on a busman's holiday with more breathless anticipation.

Miss B., looking just as "the doctor" had described her, was at the desk. I gave her my note of introduction, murmuring something vague and, I hope, polite about the honor it had been to meet Doctor Smith and how he had suggested I call. She looked at me, at the three of us, a little quizzically, I thought.

"Doctor—Doctor Smith, you say?" She still was eying me as she slit the envelope and took out the note. Then, as she read, to my horror I saw her shoulders begin to shake. In another second she was looking at me again, but now her eyes twinkled and she rocked with helpless laughter.

"Why, that old rascal," she chuckled when she could control her voice. "Doctor Alex Smith, indeed! Alex has been our night watchman for more than twenty years! He's on vacation and is spending it with relatives somewhere in New Jersey. We all love him in spite of his irritating sense of humor, but this—just wait until he gets back!"

Yes, Miss B. did show us through the hospital; but, no, I did *not* mention the other letter of introduction to Doctor C. The watchman had had his fun and I was taking no more chances. But never in all the years since then have I been allowed to forget Doctor Alex Smith, specialist in practical jokes.

The longer I fly the more convinced I become that every plane in the air is a cross section in miniature of all humanity. All the joys and sorrows, all the beauty and ugliness, the gradations in human character, all these are to be found aboard the planes sliding across the arc of heaven. And the element of surprise is there always.

Some experiences that have elements of high comedy in them are suspiciously close to tragedy when weighed dispassionately. Some are just funny. In the early days traveling by air was not the silent, soothing, slipping through the skyways it is today; it was a noisy business at best and the air lines furnished passengers with little packets containing cotton wads to put in their ears, and gum to chew to ventilate them. Once when I was traveling on the southwest division, two Indians boarded the plane at Oklahoma City traveling to Dallas. Conservatively dressed, speaking good English, they accepted the little traveling aids without comment. Then they quietly discarded the cotton wads and used the gum in their place! All a matter of taste, I guess.

On a nine o'clock flight from New York to Chicago back in the late thirties an attractive young mother boarded the plane. She was loaded with all the awkward paraphernalia necessary to traveling with a baby, and directly behind her came an elderly man carrying the baby, a child of about eighteen months. I suggested they take the front seat where there was more leg room.

The man handed the baby to its mother and then while I looked on, practically in a state of shock, he removed his overcoat, suit coat, suspenders, shoes and—dentures! These last he dropped into the magazine rack. I tried not to look at his wife who seemed just as anxious to avoid my eyes, and as other passengers were arriving, I left the strange family and went about my duties. When we were airborne I couldn't help noticing that the elderly "husband" replaced all his impedimenta and came aft to the Blue Room.

I was busy serving breakfast and the last one to be served, due to the seating, was the young mother. I placed the baby in the vacant seat on the aisle, served the mother her breakfast and said, "I have a seat farther back for your husband if he would like it—it won't be so crowded."

Never shall I forget that young woman's expression as she looked up at me with a troubled, rueful smile. "But he's *not* my husband," she said. "I've never laid eyes on him before! The porter deposited all my luggage around me at the airport and left. I guess this man must have been watching because just as I was beginning to wonder how I was going to manage with the baby and everything, he simply appeared out of thin air, took the baby from me and said, 'I'm on that flight. I'll carry the baby if you can manage the other things.' What could I do? He seemed so kindly and I certainly didn't want to make a scene, but now I don't know how to rid myself of him."

"Are you going all the way to Chicago? And how far is he going? Did he tell you?" This was an odd situation and I didn't like it.

"Fortunately," she answered, "I'm going only as far as Cleveland where my husband is meeting me, and he, the man, is going to Chicago. By the way, what has become of him?"

"He must still be in the Blue Room." Even as I answered, it suddenly dawned on me that he had been there for almost an hour. Had he been taken ill? A heart attack? Had he died? I gave my Blue Room key to one of the men passengers and asked him if he would mind looking to see what, if anything, was wrong. He was back in a few seconds.

"Believe it or not," he said, "but he's in there washing his socks!"

After a while the strange man came out, water oozing gently over his shoe tops. When we arrived at Cleveland he waved to the baby as I carried it to the door, but made no move to help the mother with her many boxes and bags. Apparently our Boy Scout felt that one good deed a day was his quota and he had filled it. It was a relief to see that sweet mother and her baby greeted by her young husband at the barrier, and I can just imagine the strange story she had to tell him.

But the strangest part of the story was yet to come. Scarcely were we airborne again, heading for Chicago, than my weird passenger once more locked himself in the Blue Room. This time I investigated myself and found him industriously washing his shirt. It took him some time and when finally he did emerge, it was in his sopping wet shirt, carrying his necktie. As he passed me on the way to his seat, he waved the tie nonchalantly at me, observing, "Have to carry this—colors might run."

All the way to Chicago I worried, and at last when we were coming in, I couldn't help saying as I helped him on with his coat, "You'd better go home quickly or you'll take cold in those wet clothes."

For just a second he eyed me a little haughtily; then he said, "Oh, I'm only out for the ride. I'm taking the midnight plane back to New York where I live."

In a way the strange incident was amusing, but obviously the man was more than simply an eccentric. Would he take the midnight plane back to New York? Was it really his home? For all its amusing aspects here was a story whose ending I never knew, and I never think of it without a shudder.

chapter 3

M Y dear old lady who was surprised at our ability to stay within what she thought were
travel lanes was not the only person to be fooled by
the navigation lights. Not long after her ride, a gentleman called me one evening and pointed from his
window. I knew what was coming for he wore
glasses and squinted badly. Sure enough.

"Don't you think someone ought to notify the
pilot, Miss?" he asked a little tremulously, pointing.
"There's another plane been riding along beside us
for fully half an hour, much too close I'd say, even
though it doesn't swerve a foot."

I explained about the navigation lights and he
relaxed, polishing his glasses, his face a bright pink.

One old gentleman of ninety-five, very hard of
hearing and quite forgetful, but the dearest soul,
made one flight particularly entertaining for every-

one aboard. "You know, young lady," he told me the moment we were airborne, "I'm ninety-five and this is my first ride in an airplane and I sure do like it!"

I said how glad we were that he was enjoying his ride, and went about my duties. Half an hour later I met him in the aisle leaning over the chair of a fellow passenger, beaming. "You know," he was shouting, "I'm in my ninety-sixth year and this is my first ride in the air, and I can't think why I didn't try it long ago. My, but it's wonderful, just wonderful!"

This song in praise of flying continued with variations throughout the trip and when finally I waved him off and saw his family greeting him, faintly I caught the now familiar words, "To think I had to be ninety-five before I had a ride in an airplane, the only way to travel, mind you, the only way!"

I shall never forget two sweet nuns who boarded the Chicago-bound *Mainliner* in San Francisco. They felt we stewardesses had far too much to do and were determined to help us serve the meals! I had to explain very carefully that such kind help would be strictly against the rules, and I hope I convinced them that our work was not nearly so heavy as they seemed to feel it was.

Flying Mary O'Connor

One of the most delightful passengers I ever had was Mrs. Franklin D. Roosevelt. She was our First Lady at the time, yet a more self-effacing, considerate person I never have known. Everything pleased her. All the passengers wanted to have at least a moment or two with her and it was wonderfully heartwarming to see how really interested she was in each individual who came to her seat. She was knitting and I remember how she never seemed to drop a stitch as she chatted with first one and then another eager passenger. Finally it was my turn and when I confessed that I'd always wanted to knit but somehow lacked the knack of making the needles do what I wanted them to, she made me sit down. Slowly and patiently she showed me the rudiments of knitting. I'm no expert today, I admit, but *I really can knit* and I owe the fact to Mrs. Roosevelt. No wonder with that generous, outgoing nature that she wins the whole world to her.

The day Will Rogers came aboard will always remain one of the most chuckly bits of nostalgia in my entire flying career. As you probably know, this great humorist and salty "cowboy philosopher" was never without his chewing gum. I'd seen him on the stage swinging his lariat in the most intricate loops, and with every flip of the rope his jaws would match the rhythm as he chomped away on his famous gum.

I had been warned, so I had several extra packs on hand. I can still see him coming up the steps to the plane, carrying a small portable typewriter. He grinned at me, waved a friendly "Howdy," and slid into a seat. There, with his hat still on the back of his head and the typewriter on his knees, he began typing away on his daily newspaper assignment.

When we were airborne I went to his seat armed with my several packs of gum and suggested he might like a fresh piece since he was already chewing busily. He looked up from his work, smiled that slow, pleasant smile of his, and shook his head.

"Thank you, no, ma'am," he said. "I never chew gum. All I ever chew is this—" and he took from his pocket several short lengths of white string!

Not long after the new year, 1940, my supervisor called me into the office to tell me about a new plan United Air Lines was just mulling over that they thought might interest me. They were thinking of giving all stewardesses "In Flight" training which would make them as nearly perfect in their jobs as possible. The last remnant of the old independent procedure, the learn-as-you-go method was to go, to be replaced by very definite regulations. Would I undertake the training job? Generously they said I'd been a good stewardess and that they did not think the girls would resent having me as that most hated being among girls, a woman boss. Would I try it?

Frankly, it was an experiment and it just might not work out, though my supervisor was kind enough to say she thought it would. It would mean that I would be the first Stewardess Flight Instructress in American aviation. I would organize my own time and the work would be fitted into that time; I was to remember, however, that should it fail there would be no returning to the rank of stewardess. What did I think? It would be a tremendous promotion if it succeeded; it could also be the end of flying for me.

Well, I was young, a terrific enthusiast, and full of confidence. Here was an opportunity to help new stewardesses and to bring prestige to the company I was serving, and I saw no reason for having the slightest reservation. Heretofore stewardesses had been more or less under the surveillance of employees of the company who had flown on business and always had turned in a routine written report on stewardess fitness when they returned to the home office. This was far from satisfactory, nor was it quite fair, since a business man was often guilty of snap judgment or no judgment at all if he happened to be tired and anxious to get home. It was a challenge and I accepted it with few misgivings.

First of all, I let the girls know that my reason for being there was not to spy on them, to criticize and go tearing back to the home office with a damaging report if things did not go right. I explained that I was there to help make their jobs easier and more pleasant and that before I sent in my report we would always take a few minutes after the flight to discuss the trip, and that if they could convince me that anything in the report was unfair I would change it.

Being completely honest and fair with the girls of the organization paid rich dividends. We trusted one another. So I became permanent Flight Instructress and a sort of Mother Confessor into the bargain. The company was pleased with the progress of the stewardesses and with the new interest they showed in their work, in the little added touches they gave their service.

It was not always easy to criticize a conscientious worker, for oddly enough it was, as a rule, the very conscientious girl who most often slipped up in some one part of her work simply because she was perfection in everything else.

A complaint had come to me almost before I had settled into the new job that Miss X. never picked up the newspapers, blankets, pillows, etc., before the flight landed, a major misdemeanor. So I watched, and certainly the criticism seemed justified. I could not believe my eyes, so I gave her the benefit of one more full flight, watching her meanwhile.

There was no doubt about it: she gave her passengers every attention during the flight, was perfect in serving the meals, was, in short, the perfect stewardess until the flight was almost over and the job at hand was for her to make the cabin—her part of it—shipshape for the landing. But not at all. Blankets flopped over chair backs, pillows were tumbled into corners, newspapers and magazines tripped you in the aisle. There was no help for it: I must speak to her and explain what I should have to put into my report.

I praised her beautiful work in flight, said how we appreciated her interest in it and in her passengers. Then I added that only one thing stood in the way of her being an absolutely perfect stewardess and that was her habit of leaving the cabin in disorder when we landed. I pointed out that if everything was orderly before landing, there would be no chance that a passenger could lose any valuables among rumpled blankets, or possibly trip over newspapers in the aisle and then sue the company if an ankle were broken or even sprained.

She said she knew she had already been reported to the Ground Office but was not sure what for.

Now she thanked me for my understanding and the good talk we had had, and promised never to be lax again—and she wasn't. She became one of the best stewardesses we had and now, eighteen years later, she holds a responsible position and is looked upon as the very acme of order and system. Whenever we meet, and we do frequently, she still beams at me and says, "I owe all my success to you, Miss O'Connor. Sensitive as I was back in those days, if you had given me a harsh talking to and told me to change my ways 'or else,' I know I would have decided I was no good at anything and dear only knows what I might have done. As it is . . ." One look at her was enough to convince anyone that here was a very successful career woman.

Then there was another girl whose very high spirits were her undoing. The child meant no harm but it seemed almost impossible to impress her with the fact that, no matter how well meaning you might be, there were still some things you just did not do. Repeatedly I warned her about too loud laughter when her naturally ebullient sense of humor betrayed her; again and again I told her that because a slight turbulence might make the plane sway a little, she was not called upon to do a gay dance step in the aisle. She tried, I'm sure she did, but in my heart I knew she was the type that no amount of patient training and talking to could change. The day came when unfortunately I was proved right. And it was a fairly unimportant incident that did it, too.

One of the men passengers had spent most of the time aboard going over a weighty manuscript. I assumed he was an editor. He was completely absorbed in it and had only a few more pages to read when we landed at La Guardia airport in New York. Automatically, he fastened his seat belt as we were coming in, and then went right on reading, hoping, I suppose, to finish the last page before we landed. The stewardess was passing out hats and coats, and when she reached his chair, instead of speaking to him, she laughingly jammed his hat on his head and walked on, calling over her shoulder, "Planning to spend the week end with us?"

It was a tiny straw, but it broke the camel's back. The man was furious and his report reached the Ground Office even before my less violent one could. That poor, bad-mannered girl was discharged. I was sorrier than I can say, but not surprised. She had been warned so often, but all to no avail. Now, since that is the way of life, she had to pay the piper. I think of her often, wonder what she is doing, wonder whether she is still romping through life, bewildered at the blows it deals her, unaware that she has only herself to blame, poor lamb.

Flying Mary O'Connor

Almost everything about flying is delightful, but occasionally by way of a bit of leavening, there come the unpleasant moments to show us that after all we are *not* merely playing parts but are holding jobs calling for certain abilities. I remember a certain flight from New York to Chicago with scheduled stops at Philadelphia and Cleveland. The meteorologist had predicted a wind shift between Cleveland and Chicago. Today we call a "wind shift" a "cold front." In those days we did not fly very high and it was unknown to fly above or around a turbulence of any kind, so the approaching "wind shift" promised some pretty spectacular bouncing around.

In Philadelphia three flighty, shrill-voiced women came aboard. They had heard of the turbulence to be expected and were making the most of their knowledge. The seven other passengers were business men, and the incessant hysterical cackling was exasperating them, I could see. Then shortly before we were due in Cleveland, the pilot called me to the cockpit with a startling bit of news: one wheel of the landing gear was stuck. He was going to circle the airfield meanwhile, trying to get it down. We would make several approaches to the field, hoping for the best. I was to use my own judgment about what to tell the passengers; and he or the co-pilot would keep me informed.

Thinking of those three women, I probably looked as though I were coming down with some obscure disease as I made my way back to the cabin. I had to act quickly as time was running out. A perfectly harmless fib seemed the most sensible thing.

I took a deep breath and began. I explained that the wind shift had moved much faster than we had anticipated and was now over Cleveland. (Incidentally, I wondered where it *really* was!) Now, I continued, praying for a convincing manner, a wind shift was also a change in wind direction. We always landed into the wind, and with the wind shifting so erratically, we might have to make several approaches to the field.

The three women accepted the story without a murmer, and as we tried one approach after another, and still that stubborn wheel stuck, there was something almost grimly amusing about the way they would turn their heads as one, squealing, "Ooooo, look, the wind's shifted again! It's from the east now; it was from the west a minute ago!"

I had quietly told the men passengers the truth meanwhile and knew I could depend upon them to be calm. Presently the pilot called me and said he was going to make the final approach and to prepare the passengers. I told them all now exactly what had happened and how to prepare for an emergency. I know this sounds incredible, but truly, you would have thought my three hysterical women had been given a mighty sedative! Suddenly they became a unit of calm stability; actually they were much calmer than the men.

We nosed down slowly, carefully, landing on one wheel, a smooth three-point landing, as the plane was steered off the runway toward soft ground. When it came to a full stop it slid quietly over on its side. No one was even slightly jarred and all my passengers, the three women giggling and screaming again, leading the way, continued on their flight to Chicago. I couldn't help thinking how often women under stress are more stable than men. Incidentally, that "wind shift" went around us and we never heard of it again.

But all stormy weather is not so easily eluded. I remember once as we were leaving Cleveland for Chicago the pilot confided that somewhere ahead we would run into a "wind shift" and that it could, as he put it, be a dilly. In those days, weather information was not as accurate as it is today, and pilots could not so easily avoid storms ahead, even when they had some advance warning. He promised to keep me informed. We were not far from Fort Wayne, Indiana, when he told me we were nearing the turbulence and that the storm was of tornado magnitude. I had the passengers fasten their seat belts and was just sitting down to fasten my own when the storm struck.

How that sturdy plane survived I shall never know. It plunged and rolled like a light tree branch caught in wild rapids; window curtains came unsnapped and flew through the air; the metal on seat belts and the legs of chairs were twisted like putty; and cushions from the few unoccupied seats danced a crazy dance down the aisle. Outside, a solid wall of sleety rain smashed into us and the wind kept up a low, hoarse roaring far more terrifying than the usual high scream of wind in a storm. This was sheer horror.

Everyone behaved very well though I'm sure none of us imagined we could possibly survive. All credit goes to our two clever pilots who managed to bring us safely down at a small airport in Lebanon, Indiana. It was used only for private planes and, as the rain slackened, cars from the town began arriving, for everyone was anxious to see the plane they had heard circling during the worst of the storm, the first commercial plane to land in their town. Hospitably they drove us into town and, as the rain and wind began again, we took the passengers to Lebanon's very attractive restaurant where the proprietor insisted on getting out gilt tables and chairs that had not been used since a visit from the Queen of Rumania some years earlier. So we made a little ceremony of what came close to being the tragic end of a journey.

Oddly enough one very seldom hears a stewardess complain of disagreeable passengers. Just why this should be so I do not know. Possibly it is because flights are short or because even today, with everyone becoming more and more blasé about traveling, there is something still new and thrilling about riding across the sky. The fault-finders are really very rare and nine times out of ten they are already in bad humor when they come aboard.

The man who complains loudly and bitterly about the service before we are off the ground probably had a tussle with the taxi driver who brought him to the airport, and he usually quiets down if you listen to him patiently, sympathetically, and perhaps hand him the morning paper and ask him if he wouldn't like a cup of coffee. Then there is the man who is taking the late afternoon flight, has tossed off "one for the road" just before arriving aboard, and is in an ugly mood. This man we let strictly alone and, as a rule, with no one to challenge his arguments, he will fall asleep. If not, then just a quiet, friendly word from the co-pilot is apt to sober him sufficiently to make him hold his tongue.

Just every now and then you will find a nervous, irritable woman who feels she is not getting all the attention she should. She cannot adjust the air vent over her chair; why isn't lunch being served? She would have had lunch at the Colony before she came if she'd had the faintest suspicion there would be no luncheon served aboard. Oh, there was? Well, then, when *would* it be served? And why couldn't she sit on the other side instead of here with the sun blazing in? Draw the curtains? No, that made it much too dark. The whole system was poor, and the only way to improve such bad service was to report it to head-quarters—beginning with the inattention of the stewardess.

There is exactly nothing you can do with such a one. You play dumb bunny, serve her as you do your other passengers—courteously, pleasantly—and keep out of her way as much as possible. Remember she probably has someone—a husband, daughter, maid—*someone* at home who cannot get away from her. Your ordeal will be over when the flight ends, so keep smiling and wave her on her way. Tomorrow will be another day.

Well, you see, flying has its seamy side like everything in life, but it is so outweighed by the fun, the adventure, that I hesitate to mention it except that I do want to be completely honest when talking about the job of a stewardess.

chapter 4

WHEN the war came, *DC 4's* and all their equipment were turned over to the government for use in the war effort. Meanwhile I was loving every split second of my life in the air. Every day was a new challenge, no two days were alike. After Pearl Harbor in December of 1941 the nursing requirement was definitely lifted and we began a whole new stewardess service. Extra First Aid courses were added to the curriculum and I began to work with each new stewardess on her first flight. There were times when I felt as though I were some sort of strange clucking bird, running around the sky like a crazy thing, not sure whether I was coming or going.

By 1943 the war was all around us, in the very air we breathed, and I began to have twinges of conscience. My country was begging for nurses and here was I, free as air, enjoying a job I loved, with no

Mary O'Connor in May 1943 on the eve of her
departure for service with the US Navy, totaling
up the number of miles she has flown

thought but to continue in it. But in the end conscience won. I asked for an early vacation that year
and took a post graduate course in nursing, bringing
me up to date, to prepare myself for service in the
Navy. In February I asked for a commission in the
Navy Nurse Corps, and United Air Lines gave me
a leave of absence as it did all personnel entering the
services. In April, I had my physical and on May 1st I
was ordered to Mare Island, California.

After three months of routine work in the surgical ward of the United States Naval Hospital at

Mare Island with about fifty patients, I was made
Senior Nurse on the Amputation Ward. Though
this may sound like a grim assignment, the rewards
were great, and never have I known such a crowd of
wonderful men. To be sure they were not angels;
they swore and they grew ugly and discouraged at
times; they even shed tears sometimes which they
tried so desperately to hide. It took them ages to be
sure I wouldn't pity them. Even the lads just out of
the operating room, minus one or both legs or arms,
would grin defiantly through drugged agony, murmuring a stale joke or grim profanity. "For crying
out loud," this pitiful bit of horseplay implied, "don't
pity me! This is nothing, really nothing at all."

I was new and they had to make sure they could
trust me. Once the ice was broken, though, we were
one big family and I was as anxious to have them
make a good impression on visiting brass as though I
actually had been their mother. And I might almost
in fact have been their mother as I grieved with them
over their multiple tragedies: the letters from someone very special back home which became fewer and
shorter and then stopped entirely; the tactless, well-
meaning letters that inadvertently told too much; the
seering humiliation of trying before the other boys
to take steps on new artificial legs—and failing.

Bitterness was the predominant characteristic

that dogged and colored their realization of what had happened to them; they were so sensitive that working with them was an education in diplomacy itself. I remember one day when a very amiable but rather insensible woman of local prominence came to visit the Ward, her object to dispense cheer and brotherly love, I believe. As she approached the bed of a lad who had lost both legs and was sunk in blackest despair, I held my breath. She assured him blithely that "it might have been worse, dear boy," and followed this bromide with, "What are you planning to do when you are discharged?"

In my wicked heart I throttled her, slapped her pretty, heavily made-up face. The sailor eyed her calmly and only his ashen pallor betrayed—to me at least—how deeply the shaft of her stupidity had gone. "I'm finding a sunny corner back home," he told her slowly, "back home where I was top pitcher for the baseball league and was pretty sure of making the big league in another year or so, and I'm going to sell pencils. Does that answer your question?"

She shook her head disapprovingly, smiled a little sadly, and turned to the boy in the next bed. "I'm sure you take a more cheerful view than your buddy here," she purred. "What are *you* going to do when you're discharged?"

This boy did not keep her waiting long. He was

a witty Texan and his bitter drawl set the whole Ward sniggering. "Me, ma'am?" he said, "why, I've got me a job already. I'm goin' to set right beside him and sharpen his pencils!" I don't think our visitor ever suspected how she had bungled, but those were some of the heartaches that endeared those men to me.

My next tour of duty, in November, was at the Bachelor Officers' Hospital, and I hadn't realized how hard it would be to say good-by to my brave amputees. However, this was war, and six months later, in May 1944, there was still another change. Seventeen girls and I were ordered to Aeia Heights, Honolulu. We traveled on a battleship and were the first women ever to be aboard one. Eight days later we docked at Honolulu and were met by the Chief Nurse and taken to Aeia Naval Hospital. There yet another six months passed, incredibly busy, often bewildering months. Then on November 13, 1944 orders came through for me to report to the Bureau of Medicine and Surgery in Washington, with priority for the first available space aboard a plane.

Miss De Witt, the Chief Nurse at the Naval Hospital, who gave me the order, had been my chief at Mare Island when first I had arrived there. She was an extraordinary woman, a wonderful nurse, and an excellent supervisor. Later she was to become Cap-

Left: Nellie Jane DeWitt, who achieved the rank of Captain in 1946 when she became Director of the Nurse Corps, US Navy. She retired in 1950. Right: Sue Dauser, who became a Captain in the Navy in 1944, and retired in 1946

tain of the entire Navy Nurse Corps. She was not by nature a particularly effusive woman, but there was something in her manner that morning in her office, a certain half-smiling restraint, as though she longed to say more but dared not.

Thirty hours later and a bit mystified, I was in Washington and had reported to the Captain of the Nurses' Corps, Captain Sue Dauser, one of this country's truly great women.

The Navy was just starting an Air Evacuation School at Alameda, California, and it developed that on the basis of my success as Flight Instructress with United Air Lines, I had been chosen by the Navy to organize and direct the Navy School of Air Evacuation! It was the first such school to be established by the Navy.

Just at the moment I could not believe the wonderful thing that had happened to me, and said so. But one look at Captain Dauser's smile told me the truth, something Miss DeWitt, I now realized, had known, too. Having been given the lowly rank of Ensign on entering the service, I was now given a spot promotion to Lieutenant (j.g.) as I would be teaching women of that rank; and there seemed almost no limit to the scope of work for which I would be directly responsible.

Now I needed all the courage, all the rather wobbly self-confidence I could muster. There were busy, almost frantic days ahead as I organized the work. Navy Evacuation planes brought in the wounded by the hundreds and I did my best to make the Navy's school of nurses and corpsmen an efficient, smoothly operating base where they could learn quickly how to care for patients in the air. Only volunteers were to be considered. One hundred and twenty-five young R.N.s would be chosen, and preference would be given to former stewardesses.

An appropriate uniform had to be selected, and as quickly as possible. I felt strongly that for the type of work the nurses would be doing, slacks would be the right costume, worn with a white blouse, and the whole designed by a clever woman with Bonwit Teller's in New York. However, Admiral McIntyre, Chief of Medicine and Surgery, to whom the design of the uniform was submitted, was not very enthusiastic. Slacks on women? Remember this was 1944. But I'm afraid my Irish tongue wagged so hard that the Admiral gave up from sheer exhaustion, for the order for slacks came through the following day and was rushed to New York.

Never did a group of young women look trimmer or more efficient than the members of the Navy Evacuation Corps. People living on the Base called them the "Navy Rockettes" and in spite of being a Lieutenant (j.g.) I found I'd been given the name of "Captain of the Navy Rockettes." It sounds a little like a corny title for a singing commercial, doesn't it?

The full course of training covered six weeks and when I think of the subjects included, the doctors lecturing, the equipment involved, it frankly makes me wonder how we did it. A run-through of what the nurses and corpsmen were drilled in will give you some idea of the scope of the work.

Mary O'Connor in the "Navy Rockette" uniform of the Navy Evacuation Corps

1. Intensive training as to the types of patients who could and could not be transported by air since some abdominal injuries do not react well to high altitudes.
2. Survival training—on water, land or jungle.
3. Loading and securing litter-borne patients while airborne.
4. How to give blood plasma to patients while in the air.
5. Use of oxygen.

6. Recognition of manifestation of oxygen want.

7. General care and comfort of patients in the air.

8. Lectures on various types of wounds, diseases, and mental cases.

9. Complete procedures for handling and ditching patients in the event of a forced landing.

Evacuation of sailors and marines from the immediate vicinity of the battlefront was important for many reasons. Getting these wounded men away from the continuous noise of bombing and the possibility of further attack was essential. A man need not be shell-shocked to be on the verge of complete nervous collapse. So one of our major efforts was to get as many neurological cases as possible away from the battle area. Also, remember, the hospitals in the forward areas were nothing more really than emergency dispensaries and could not be manned by a full staff, so anyone in need of a serious operation— an amputation, for instance—that could be delayed for twenty-four hours, was flown to this country for the necessary surgery.

The mental cases were among our gravest problems because, I hate admitting it, some boys would feign a mental breakdown in order to be invalided home. This wasn't good, certainly, but it was none-theless understandable when one considered the weeks, even months, of horror they had been living through. It was our job to talk them out of permitting this stigma to appear on their war records and often it was an almost impossible task.

Then there were the boys with nerve injuries requiring special surgery, others awaiting amputations, and still others—leukemia victims as a rule—in poor condition, who were rushed to Naval hospitals near their homes. But the lads for whom my heart ached particularly were those whose terrible wounds refused to heal and who had to be forwarded to larger hospitals for plastic surgery. It was through their suffering, I think, that the full horror and futility of *all* war impressed itself upon me.

My enthusiasm for the Air Evacuation work nearly equalled my love for the months spent with the amputees back on Mare Island. There were twelve planes to each of the three squadrons operating in and out of the Base, each manned with two corpsmen and two nurses, and the work those dedicated young men and women did was magnificent. I counted it an honor to be associated with them.

Most of the flying was done at night or in the very early morning hours and fully ninety-five percent of the flights were over water. There were domestic flights, too, bringing critical cases to hospitals nearer their homes, and carrying mental patients to the fine mental hospitals at Fort Worth. Again, others were being transferred to hospitals where specialized treatment could be given. The days, the nights were filled with the long saga of pain.

Then the war was mercifully over, in 1945, and the training school was closed in August of that year, though evacuations of patients continued well into 1946. I wish I could describe just how, even in retrospect, I still feel about those war years. They were unique, years that added a balance and a leaven to the rather offhand buoyancy of my outlook on life up to that time. I seemed to have turned a corner now and to be banking—coming in for a beautiful landing at a new and glamorous base.

chapter 5

NOW that the war was over, men and women who had been in the forefront of its tempest found themselves suddenly superfluous, trying to adjust to peace-time living. Planes still brought in the wounded, boys coming home at last, and for another year I arranged schedules, checked the nurses and corpsmen on flight, and worked some flights across the country with patients myself. Slowly, gradually, the evacuation lessened and finally came to a stop.

I was offered the position of Chief Stewardess with Western Airlines and at the same time the Navy tendered a permanent commission. This was all very gratifying and I did appreciate it, but I never had thought of a military career, and if I were to continue flying I knew it would be with the company that had given me my start, United.

Flying back East I found myself thinking of

the years that had passed since that morning back in '33 when I had boarded a plane for the first time. They had been full years, wonderfully happy years. But for a decision I had made during that first month of flying, I might never have known how packed with the real joy of accomplishment life can be. One of the strict rules of the stewardess job is that no stewardess may marry and still hold her position with the airlines. And at that time a lad with a will as strong as my own told me that either I would give up flying at once and marry him or our engagement would end. I still cannot believe the decision was so simple to make. Give up flying? Why, flying was my whole life!

That had been thirteen years ago. Had I ever regretted my choice? Never. Through the years there had been many wonderfully pleasant friendships with men whose sincere regard I know I shall always have; during the war hospital days there were lonely, homesick boys who inevitably fell in love, or thought they did, with their nurse, and then there were the weird characters every girl in the business or professional field meets sooner or later.

Back in the early days a man boarded my plane in San Francisco bound for New York. He was a chatty soul, almost impossible to discourage, and made much of the fact that we had the same name, O'Connor. It didn't strike me as anything to send up red flares about since O'Connor is part of the Smith-Jones-Brown group and a great many of them have come my way. This particular Mr. O'Connor was something of a nuisance, however, as he persisted in telling me about his love life. He was a gambler by profession, spent most of his time in Las Vegas, and at the moment was in despair, he said, because the girl he wanted to marry had gone back East, saying she would have nothing further to do with him unless he gave up gambling and got a legitimate position. He was on his way East to try to persuade her to return to Las Vegas with him. With all my heart I hoped she would have the good sense not to!

Mr. O'Connor was among the passengers to change planes at Chicago and just before we landed, as I walked through the plane reminding passengers to fasten their seat belts, he stopped me.

"Miss O'Connor," he said with a perfectly straight face, "I've been sitting here thinking it over. Why don't you marry me? You'd not even have to change your name, so no one would be the wiser and you could go right on flying and I could go back to Las Vegas. Together we could have a wonderful life!"

I wanted to say, "Wonderful for whom?" but a stewardess does not do that. So I told my harebrained, double-dealing Romeo good-by and wished him well.

While I was still chuckling over that foundered romance, I suddenly remembered another, this one a proposal by mail. The writer said he was fifty years old and admitted he was not bad looking. He lived at a Veterans' Hospital, was unable to work much, and would prefer to live in the country where he could have a sports car to drive. He wanted an amiable wife who would be entertaining and had traveled and knew the ways of the world. Would I be interested? He did not say who was to maintain the country home and the sports car.

So, smiling over the amusing little twists in human nature, I looked out and down and there was Lake Michigan shimmering in the early morning sunshine. I had come home!

At first nothing seemed to have changed, yet some things had: there were new faces and some of the old ones were gone. The word *"Mainliner"* kept creeping into conversations and so I learned that our beautiful big planes had just been named *"Mainliners"* early in 1946. The name had been copyrighted and permission had been given the Ford Motor Company to give their new model car the same name. *Mainliner*—I liked the name.

Oh, but it was good to be home again! It seemed

strange being processed through the familiar Person-nel Office, but changes in stewardess training had come and if I were to serve the company in any capacity I must be brought up to date on new pro-cedures in passenger service. And at once I was put to work writing a new Stewardess Manual. With the new duties that were waiting, it was a year before I had the Manual in satisfactory form.

And those new duties? Mr. William A. Patter-son, President of United Air Lines, was to make an inspection trip to Mexico to satisfy himself about Lamsa Air Lines, a subsidiary of United flying be-tween El Paso and "south of the border," and asked me to act as stewardess. Mr. Patterson is one of the most beloved men in the field of flying and naturally I was delighted to have the opportunity of making the Mexican flight, eager to prove that my years with the Navy had not dulled my enthusiasm for com-mercial flying. The trip was perfect right down to its last pleasant little surprise.

"Mary," Mr. Patterson said as we were coming into Chicago, "we've been in the process of setting up an official plane—you may have heard talk of it around the office—and it occurred to me you might like to be my personal stewardess." His eyes were twinkling and he added, chuckling, "Guess I'll call the plane the 'Mary O'Connor.' Does the job strike

William A. Patterson, President of United Air Lines

you? You'd be responsible for the In Flight, for management of the plane, attending to all details, you know. There'll be times when I'll use the plane as my office between cities; sometimes there'll be guests whether I'm aboard or not. I'd want you to see that everything was done as perfectly as you would do it in your own home. I've talked the whole thing over with the officers and they like the idea. What do you say, Mary?"

What did I say? What *could* I say? I was horribly afraid if I so much as opened my mouth I'd blubber. I think I made it clear to Mr. Patterson though that nothing in my whole life ever had given me such a wonderful surprise, that nothing could make me happier than the thought of being Senior Stewardess in charge of United's Executive plane. Only once in an assortment of lifetimes, I told myself, could anything so fine happen to any girl. And through the years since that day late in '46 I have been proved so right.

That was in mid-winter. The following May I made a flight aboard the new *Executive Mainliner* to San Francisco with a group of our officials, and as I walked slowly down its length before my passengers arrived, I fairly caught my breath at its beauty. It contained a galley with an extra table for working and serving space, and drawers for linens. Beyond a partition were two Pullman sections with double seats, two facing aft and two forward, with removable table for use if needed. These two compartments could be made into two sleeper compartments of two berths each, an upper and a lower. In the main cabin, separated from the sleeping compartments by an-

Mary O'Connor aboard the *Executive Mainliner*

other partition, there were a deep davenport to seat three, and five comfortable club chairs—one a swivel. Behind this was a desk with a typewriter and beyond were the cloakroom and lavatory. It was perfect.

We were to leave for Los Angeles the following morning after spending the night in San Francisco and I was up in plenty of time to reach the airport at seven o'clock. I was still dressing when the phone rang and the co-pilot called to tell me they were being held up with some minor trouble so I was not needed until eight instead of seven. Well, that was that, though we so seldom had any mechanical trouble while on a trip that I wondered a little.

When I arrived at the airport I wondered even more, for there sat our beautiful *Mainliner* with all the officials standing, looking very pleased with themselves, gazing up at her nose. On the side of the nose of every *Mainliner* was a circle inside of which was the United shield. Around the top of the circle was the word "*Mainliner*" and now as I hurried forward I could not help seeing what had been freshly painted around the bottom of the circle: the word "O'Connor." It had never entered my mind that Mr. Patterson was serious when he had spoken of calling the Executive plane the O'Connor. He had

Mary O'Connor and the *Mainliner O'Connor*, 1946

spoken so casually, almost in fun, it seemed, yet here it was!

"How do you like it, Mary?" he called and the others joined in a laughing, applauding chorus. Ah, this time there were no words. How could anyone who did not *really* believe in leprechauns expect me to believe what I saw? Never a word would force itself past my lips—never a one. It would have drowned if it had in the foolish cascade spilling down my cheeks.

That first beautiful *Mainliner O'Connor* offered hospitality in the air to many famous people and to several who were gravely ill and were being flown home or to hospitals. Ex-President Hoover came aboard on his eightieth birthday (1954) and I never have had a more delightful or more thoughtful passenger. Mr. Hoover was in Cedar Rapids for the celebration; the day was hot and humid, and as I knew there would be no ground air cooler in this small intermediate station—we had ferried over from Chicago—I turned on all the cold air to have the cabin cool and comfortable when he arrived.

However, he was tired and very warm when he came aboard and fearing he might take cold because of the drastic change in temperature, I put a pretty blue blanket around his shoulders and another across his knees. I know it pleased him for he smiled

Ex-President Herbert Hoover

his very special cherubic smile and said, "This is very nice, very nice, indeed."

In his party were Bob Considine and three secretaries, these latter to look after the huge bag of congratulatory letters and telegrams Mr. Hoover had received on his birthday.

With his lunch I had a pretty cupcake with one

candle on it brought in for dessert. I knew he would have had a very special cake in Iowa and said so, and added that we still wanted to add *our* bit to the celebration. Again there was that twinkling smile, the expression of genuine delight at having been remembered. He admitted then a little ruefully that he had had *six* birthday cakes but that as his doctor had forbidden him all sweets, he knew that no one would be hurt if he did not taste them, delicious though they looked, including the little United cupcake. A more lovable passenger never stepped aboard the *Mainliner O'Connor* and the entire crew lost its collective heart.

After lunch Mr. Hoover began to dictate answers to all his birthday letters, dividing the dictation among the three secretaries, and the following day they told me he had dictated right through to midnight, stopping only for dinner, and then had begun again at nine in the morning. (The gracious letter I received is among my most prized possessions.)

The head secretary told me such an illuminating thing about Mr. Hoover's character and I think it is worth repeating for the benefit of those who may mistakenly feel that a brilliant and celebrated person must necessarily be callous in his dealings with lesser folk. She said the first day she was called to his office eighteen years earlier, to take his dictation, she was

HERBERT HOOVER

The Waldorf Astoria Towers
New York, New York
August 20, 1954

My dear Miss O'Connor:

This is just to register my

appreciation and admiration of a great

lady -- one Mary O'Connor.

With kind regards,

Yours faithfully,

Herbert Hoover

Miss Mary O'Connor
c/o The Mainliner O'Connor
United Air Lines
Chicago, Illinois

so overcome with stage fright that not one word of what he said registered! She sat, making dots and dashes, frantically praying for courage to say, "Please, sir, I cannot keep up," yet afraid to open her mouth. This went on for well over an hour. Finally, Mr. Hoover said, "That will be all for today, thank you. Are you sure you have everything?"

She said yes, she was sure and went to her desk, her mind a complete blank. For a few moments she sat, trying to remember, to reconstruct even one sentence of what she was supposed to have written, but it was no use. Nothing would come. Nothing. Now in a blind panic she hurried back to Mr. Hoover's office and blurted out the truth.

Instead of scorn or impatience she found a friend who simply said, "Sit down. I understand. Nerves can play us tricks. Now we'll begin again." And he re-dictated the entire sheaf of letters—which she took down this time with no trouble at all. She has been his chief secretary ever since, a position she would not change for any other on earth. Mr. Hoover, she says, is a man whose natural gentle dignity is far too often mistaken for austerity, and his great modesty often acts as a barrier to the more obvious forms of public homage.

During both of the Eisenhower campaigns we were privileged to have Mr. Eisenhower and Mr.

Nixon as our passengers a number of times. Mr.
Eisenhower has a keen, quiet sense of humor and
seems most at home when he is with a small group
of his colleagues, talking over plans, often laughing
at jokes on himself. Watching any group of which

Ex-President
Dwight D. Eisenhower

President (then Senator)
John F. Kennedy with
Ex-Vice President
Richard M. Nixon

he is a part, one can see instantly in what affectionate regard he is held by all his associates. I never heard him raise his voice in a peremptory request or challenge. In my own mind I've always thought of him as a man of peace, a man to whom good will meant far more than a noisy accolade of triumph for destructive battles won, a man who does really love his fellow men.

I like to think of the group of elderly Mormons, charming men and women all of them, whom we carried as part of their Centennial celebration across the country they or their ancestors traveled in covered wagons from Salt Lake City to Nauvoo, Illinois. The youngest passenger was eighty-two, the oldest ninety-four, and I've never seen a more enthusiastic group of people. They seemed to savor every single mile of the route, pointing, exclaiming. The cabin fairly tinkled with little shrieks of recognition from the ladies as we flew low over certain familiar landmarks, and with laughing shouts of, "Remember when . . .?" from the men. It was a great day for that happy band of Latter Day Saints.

One lady told me of the trip her family made across the plains in a covered wagon when they were attacked by Indians. Her mother, brothers, and sisters all were killed and their supplies taken by the savages. She and her father were somehow overlooked in the melee. It is heartbreaking to consider that poor father's situation as he buried his beloved dead and then set out with his little four-year-old daughter from a spot near Omaha and walked to Salt Lake City.

The trek covered six months, "and," the intrepid little lady finished her story, "you know, I think those weary miles decided me right then and there that one day I'd have some sort of transportation of my own. I'm eighty-seven, and a couple of years ago I got around to buying myself a bicycle. I do love a good baseball game and now I can ride to and from every one—never miss a game!" How is that for spirit?

Brigham Young's youngest daughter, his fifty-second child, was one of the party, a perfectly delightful woman who had any number of fascinating stories to tell about her father. All told, it was one of the most entertaining flights I ever had.

There are always deep-dyed reasons for employee loyalty and when one considers only a few of the magnificent examples of good will demonstrated by certain organizations one can the better understand the loyalty of their employees to them. As an example: there was the case of one of our pilots who just at the end of the war developed appendicitis while near Wake Island. He was a gravely sick young man. A young surgeon operated and our pilot came home healthy and beaming.

Out of gratitude, Mr. Patterson wrote the young surgeon and said if at any time United Air Lines could be of service to him he had only to let us know. Slightly less than a year later the doctor called us to say he was being transferred to Hawaii. His young wife was eight months pregnant and as the Army could not take the responsibility of transporting her under the circumstances, he wondered if we had anything to suggest. It was imperative that she go with him because there was a two-year-old boy as well, and no one with whom to leave him. Once in Hawaii, the father felt he would be able to make a satisfactory arrangement for his family.

Mainliner O'Connor was put at their disposal at once and this time I acted the dual part of stewardess and nurse should the necessity arise. We had a perfect flight and I lost my heart not only to the young mother but to her small son as well. The doctor had not realized that not only the Army planes but commercial air lines as well do not carry women passengers under similar circumstances. So bless *Mainliner O'Connor* for her status as a semi-private plane and Mr. Patterson for his generosity in lending her.

Another time, Mr. Patterson loaned his plane

to the American Cancer Society when it was conducting a campaign to raise funds for research, and was, at the same time, carrying out an educational campaign. Many celebrities of stage, screen, radio, and television donated their time and talents to the cause, traveling on Mr. Patterson's *Mainliner.* As usual, I was the stewardess, and received a Certificate of Appreciation from the Society, for taking care of all of these people during the flight.

Just recently United Air Lines played a major part in one of the greatest feats in plastic surgery ever undertaken in this country—or any other so far as I have ever heard. A little three-year-old girl living in Providence, Rhode Island, suffered seventy-three percent burns on her body, sixty-five percent of which were third-degree. The fingers and thumb of her right hand were gone and there was talk of amputating the arm. Grafts of the mother's skin had been taken without success, and the child hovered on the borderline between life and death. Her father was in Long Beach, California, and for some reason was unable to go to the child.

I was in Philadelphia where Mr. Patterson had gone on business and a call came through for me from a former Navy friend, Doctor Harold LeBlond in Long Beach. The little girl's father was asking to have his skin used on the off chance that it might save his child's life. Doctor LeBlond was willing to undertake the delicate operation of so much skin removal if in some way it could be transported successfully such a great distance to the patient who was to receive it. Obviously she was too ill to be moved. Was there, he asked, anything United Air Lines could do to help? The skin would be shipped in a gallon thermos container with a cover of hyperthermia plastic refrigeration packed with ice and kept in Saint Mary's Hospital in Long Beach until flight time.

Now this is the sort of challenge Mr. Patterson loves. In a few minutes the wires were humming in all directions. Our Traffic Manager in Long Beach was alerted; the hospital in Providence readied its staff; at Chicago, where a change would have to be made, the whole ground force received orders—priority orders.

The operation on the father was performed successfully and the precious cargo was started on its way east. A difference of ten percent in temperature had been allowed, but the skin arrived in Providence in perfect condition with a change of less than four percent! The child, for the first time since her terrible injuries, received a skin graft that "took." She was out of danger and would live.

It is things like this that make me so proud to be associated with air service in any form and especially with a man like Mr. Patterson who quietly brushes aside any part he may have had in it with a modest, "Oh, it was just one of those things." Here is part of a letter we received from Doctor LeBlond which gives some idea of the magnitude of the whole undertaking:

". . . I will someday send you clippings of the end results of the work that was initiated for the first time with your help. Without it, it never could have been accomplished. Your Doctor Wagner and your manager, Mr. Connell, did a tremendous piece of work in helping solve some of the problems that confronted us. This was the first time a skin graft had been taken and sent trans-continentally and placed on a recipient with the time lapse and the distance that were involved. Mr. Connell went out to the airport to make sure that the unit in which the grafts were packed arrived aboard and were placed under as ideal conditions as possible. Throughout the week he gave me help and advice and then the dovetailing of the schedules in Chicago and the arrival in Providence allowed the doctors there to be in surgery and ready to go at the time the grafts arrived. . . . This is the first time in surgical history, and I will have to give most of the credit where it belongs, with you, Mr. Patterson, and your staff, for the help they gave us."

One longs to be free to throw open the files to show the letters of praise and affectionate regard that poured in to us from doctors, nurses, townspeople, the child's parents and relatives, even from far away places—for so does word of a good deed travel.

Harold Stassen, handsome, dynamic, and unfailingly courteous, made the trip between Chicago and Alexandria, Minnesota with us several times. Obligingly he autographed the *Mainliner O'Connor's* guest book thus: "Best wishes always to Mary O'Connor and *the O'Connor*."

I think often of the late Wendell Willkie and

Wendell L. Willkie and Mrs. Willkie, during his Presidential campaign

the mobs of newspaper men who seemed to hem him in whenever he came aboard, though this was long before the days of the *Mainliner*. If my memory serves me correctly, it was in 1936, and he was a Senator from Indiana. I was the stewardess on the plane that flew him and the press around the country on his Presidential Campaign. There was something so vital about that extraordinary man, something so earnest and eager. He seemed a very bundle of energy with so much more that he wanted to accomplish than ten men could possibly achieve in a lifetime. He seemed to me a brilliant man, years ahead of his time. I always had the feeling that even taking time off for one of our fabulous lunches or dinners seemed a waste of time to him, though he never failed to compliment us, often mentioning some special dish he had enjoyed.

Back in 1955 when Gregory Peck came East for the premiere of *Moby Dick* at New Bedford, Massachusetts, the *Mainliner O'Connor* for three days became "The Moby Dick Special" and we were kept busy flying press, radio, and television representatives and guests from the Coast for the big event. It was the gayest June I can remember.

And speaking of motion picture people, John Wayne and his wife, Pilar, and the late Ward Bond and his wife were four who endeared themselves to me at once, maybe because they were so enthusiastic about the *Mainliner O'Connor*. They loved her and her service, thought she was beautiful, perfectly equipped, loved the meals, were ecstatic about everything we did. Truly, it was like having a party in your own home because those dear, friendly people insisted that you join their rollicking fun throughout the day. They made you forget they were celebrities; they were your guests enjoying themselves. I found myself wondering who was entertaining whom! A year later the Waynes stopped over in Chicago on their way to Europe and tele-

Above: Gregory Peck, Mary O'Connor, John Huston, Frederick
Ledebur; Below: Pilar Wayne, John Wayne, Mrs. Bond, the late
Ward Bond

Mary O'Connor and Jimmy Stewart

phoned just to say "Hello." No one must blame me
for having become a name dropper as a result.

James (Jimmy) Stewart is another hero of the
screen who is a great favorite of mine. I remember
at the time of the premiere of *The Spirit of St. Louis*
he traveled aboard the *Mainliner O'Connor* and
every member of the crew was struck by his warmth
and easy friendliness with everyone. At the premiere
he insisted upon having the crew of the *Mainliner*

O'Connor in the receiving line and introduced us to his friends as they went through the line. We'll all remember that gala evening.

And somehow you know that Jimmy, the idol of the screen, is just as fine in the role of family man. Mrs. Stewart—Gloria—and the four children—two fine boys and the cunning twin girls—flew with us from Los Angeles to Akron, Ohio, and what a sweet family they were! The children were lively, happy youngsters, but so beautifully behaved, a tribute to their parents who obviously put parenthood and its responsibilities above the glamour of the screen.

There was never a dull moment aboard the *Mainliner O'Connor* as she serenely, majestically sped across the heavens. One of her most distinguished passengers was Konrad Adenauer, Chancellor of West Germany. This great man, looking far less than his impressive age, had his lovely young daughter and his son with him, and as my vacation was not far off, they suggested that I return to Germany with them. My vacation plans had been pretty well organized but it was simple to change them and soon I was on my way to Germany aboard a majestic *Lufthansa*, with the Adenauers, three of this world's most engaging people. Bonn was their destination, but I continued on to both West and East Berlin, Düsseldorf, and on through the fairy-tale Rhine

Chancellor Konrad Adenauer of West Germany (center), with his daughter and son (striped tie). Robert E. Johnson, United's senior vice president-sales and advertising, is shaking the Chancellor's hand. Directly behind Mr. Johnson (partial view) is Mayor Richard Daley of Chicago

country. All the way I kept pinching myself, thinking that but for the fact that Germany's man of the hour had elected to travel aboard the *O'Connor* I might have been, at this moment, visiting relatives in the Middle West!

Encouraged by this glorious vacation, I went the following year to Ireland and fell in love with it—a country so green, so warm with friendliness that I hated to leave it. I still get a bit teary thinking of the morning I left Limerick. I was having breakfast in a tiny restaurant near the railway station, thinking I had ample time, when suddenly travelers at a nearby table picked up their bags and started for the door, saying that the train was leaving. It didn't seem possible because I'm usually very sure of my timetables. However, I began to rummage for my purse, and to gather up my bags, when the proprietor came by my table.

"Now take your time, ma'am," he said, "and have another spot of hot tea. They'll not leave without you." Then he went to the door and shouted, "Hold it, Mike. A lady here hasn't finished her tea. What's your hurry?"

So the train from Limerick stood quietly panting on the track while I finished my tea. And I had the feeling that the proprietor and the engineer both would have been hurt if I hadn't.

So many pleasant things were happening! There were other vacations, weeks spent in Honolulu, still others in New England. Then the American Woman's Association presented me with the Earhart medal for—I quote from the plaque—"her devotion to aviation evidenced by the five million miles in her flight log, a dynamic challenge to women

AMERICAN WOMAN'S

ASSOCIATION   THE BARCLAY   111 East Forty-Eighth Street   NEW YORK 17

AMERICAN WOMAN'S ASSOCIATION

IS HONORED TO PRESENT THE EARHART MEDAL TO —

LT. MARY O'CONNOR

FOR HER DEVOTION TO AVIATION EVIDENCED BY THE FIVE MILLION MILES
IN HER FLIGHT LOG, A DYNAMIC CHALLENGE TO WOMEN ENTERING THE
FIELD OF AVIATION TODAY; FOR HER CONTRIBUTION IN ORGANIZING AND
DIRECTING THE ORIGINAL SCHOOL FOR AIR EVACUATION AT ALAMEDA
DURING HER THREE YEAR WAR SERVICE IN THE NAVY NURSE CORPS.

MEDAL IS A MINIATURE OF THE MEDAL OF THE MONTH AMELIA EARHART
PLACQUE, DESIGNED BY BRENDA PUTNAM.

entering the field of aviation today; for her contribution in organizing and directing the original school for air evacuation at Alameda during her three years war service in the Navy Nurse Corps."

Another award was the Aviation Woman's Award of the year "for outstanding accomplishment in aviation across the years." It just did not seem possible that these generous rewards for work I loved should be coming my way.

The first *Mainliner O'Connor* was replaced by a new and more efficient model, this one with a compact office in which were a desk, typewriter, dictaphone, and ship-to-shore telephone and an AM-FM radio. Time was flying on.

Above: Mary O'Connor, with six other outstanding women in aviation, received the Amelia Earhart medal in 1957. Next to Miss O'Connor, holding the original plaque, is Dorothea Hopfer, President of the American Women's Association; Below: Mary O'Connor, with Mr. and Mrs. Patterson in Honolulu

chapter 6

LET'S talk a little about your job as a stewardess if you are considering that as a career.

If anyone asked me to define an enthusiast, I know that without even stopping for breath I'd say, "An enthusiast is a person who spends more time than he should defending the object of his enthusiasm." So when someone says, "Mary, just what is there about being a stewardess that is so far ahead of any other job in the world?" I begin to bristle.

It is the sort of thing people will ask regardless of *what* your job may be if you have been letting yourself go on pretty enthusiastically about it. Take the girl who has a yen to own and operate a greenhouse and who spends her waking hours either poring over seed catalogues or reading up on soil conservation. The friend who hasn't the faintest notion about what a *Primalaceae* or a *Bellis perennis* is, is the one who will give it as her opinion that "After all, anybody can dig in the dirt. What do you see in it?"

Again, the girl who is studying medicine gets more than her share of booing from the side lines. "But why medicine?" this contingent wants to know, adding, "It's so full of horrors!" So it is not surprising that the stewardess, happy in her work, proud of her uniform, should come in for her share of discouraging criticism which takes many forms.

The first jab comes as a rule from an old classmate of her mother's. "But, my dear child," this one laments, "it's such a—a—well, forgive me, dear, but it strikes me as such a *bold* career. Don't you think so, honestly? All that business of waiting on men as well as women; being on such informal, chatty terms with the pilots—I feel your dear mother doesn't like it very much, though she's too determined not to spoil anything for you to mention it."

Of course you count ten. Then very carefully you point out some of the salient truths about a stewardess's job. In the first place, it takes a "bold" girl to make her career "bold" in the sense the old lady implied, and no "bold" girl is hired as a stewardess. If through some inadvertence such a one has been hired, she does not last long with United Air Lines or any other reputable line. Stewardesses are known for their faultless manners, so no stigma of indecorous behavior has ever been known to touch one. Pilots for the most part are serious-minded men who are fathers of growing families. Their association with the stewardesses is one of friendly camaraderie, nothing more. If he is single, a pilot may not even date one of the stewardesses while on duty, since this is strictly against company rules.

There is another criticism one hears frequently, and this, too, usually comes from an elderly, well-meaning friend-of-the-family. "It would seem to me," this one is apt to object, "that traveling about that way, so completely on your own, you would be perfect prey for unprincipled men, wolves out to make trouble for an attractive girl traveling alone."

This is just as silly and almost as common as the first criticism. No wolf is going to bother a girl who attends strictly to her own affairs—and stewardesses do. She is safer in an airplane than she would be in the Public Library.

The greatest bugbear is the most obvious one: the danger of flying. Now this is something toward which the public is very rapidly changing its whole attitude. Planes are inspected and overhauled regularly. The pilots, and the others who comprise the crew, are highly skilled, dependable men who take pride in their records. As to weather hazards, today, guided by radar, planes travel around and above even the ugliest turbulence, so that potential danger, that old time bugbear of the airways, is cut to a minimum. There are accidents in the air, yes, just as there are motor accidents and accidents to pedestrians crossing a street. Yet we do not give up driving and we do venture on foot across Times Square.

One is five times safer aboard a plane than in an automobile. Guiding the one are the pilot and co-pilot; in an automobile, only one person is in control (if one overlooks the back-seat driver)—and that person has not undergone the rigorous training required of pilots. Both conveyances are the finest examples of modern engineering workmanship, with the plane having the added advantage of superior speed. There is no safer, cleaner, more rewarding, more broadening or enjoyable work in the world for a girl than that of being a stewardess aboard a modern air liner.

A great deal has changed in the matter of training. The old casual, rather hit-or-miss training is a thing of the past. In its place are schools whose curricula include subjects like meteorology, communications, principles of aeronautics, and other technical subjects. Students are taught to walk gracefully, remembering always that posture is an important part of good looks; they learn to answer intelligently questions on geography, transportation connections, and routings. They are taught how to help mothers traveling with tiny babies and how to dispense meals efficiently and calmly twenty thousand feet in the air. They are indoctrinated with the fine rudiments of behavior by which a girl may be gracious, friendly, cheerful, without ever lowering the bars of professional rectitude. The pioneer "sky girl" is gone forever, replaced by the poised and soignée stewardess of today.

How to get such a job? United Air Lines receives an average of fifty thousand applications in a single year and for every one accepted, one hundred and fifty are rejected, so you can readily see that the standards are high. (Incidentally, the R.N. requirement was dropped after Pearl Harbor.)

Let's get down to cases and go over today's *musts*. Ask yourself the following questions and be honest with the answers you dredge up from your conscience. If most of them are "Yes," then the chances of your being accepted are good.

1. Are you between twenty and twenty-seven years of age?
2. Are you between 5'2 and 5'8?
3. Do you weigh not less than one hundred pounds and not more than one hundred and thirty-eight pounds in proportion to your height?
4. Are you single?
5. Is your general health perfect?
6. Is your vision excellent?
7. Is your hearing good?

8. Have you straight, even teeth and are they your own?

9. Is your general appearance pleasing?

10. Do you take pride in being perfectly groomed?

11. Have you a good figure?

12. Is your hair short, clean, and well styled?

13. Are your hands soft and white?

14. Do you keep your nails manicured?

15. Are you careful about your makeup—not too much?

16. Are you an R.N.? Have you a college degree? Have you had two years of college? Or have you had two years of business experience in which you had to deal with the public?

17. Are you poised?

18. Are you patient and tolerant?

19. Do you maintain a calm, serene manner under stress?

20. Are you a good conversationalist?

21. Are you able to speak easily to a group of strangers?

22. Are you a good listener? Alert?

23. Do you like children and do they like you?

24. Do you make it a point to read one newspaper a day and one book of quality a month?

I know that is rather a frightening list, but it

will give you some idea of how very careful we are in selecting our stewardesses. Some applicants are rejected because of nothing more faulty than extreme shyness. Again a girl may by nature be over-aggressive. Yet each is a characteristic which is unacceptable in a stewardess.

We began this chapter with a word about enthusiasm. Well, the airways bristle with it, and there is some resulting comedy and now and then a well-defined rumble of annoyance from several quarters. The case in point goes back to my Stewardess Flight Instructress days and perhaps I should have mentioned it then.

One of our regular commuters was a noted physicist who frequently lectured at cities on our route. He made notes on little scraps of paper. With these leading questions or observations as a guide, he would sit through the entire flight of several hours, looking out the window, silently rehearsing his lecture. He declared he always was letter-perfect by the time he reached his destination.

One day when I was not on duty he came aboard, settled back, and as soon as the plane was airborne, turned his face to the window and began his silent rehearsal. A new stewardess, whom I shall call Margaret, was in charge, a lovely girl who did all her work with a kind of dedicated zeal that I felt would take her far. Well, somewhere along the line someone must have told her how much he appreciated her efforts to help him pass the time during the flight. Margaret took it much to heart and now she could not bear to watch a lone man staring stonily out the window, not moving a muscle, obviously, her gentle nature prompted, eager for company.

This would never do. As a personal representative of United Air Lines she would change all this. He must enjoy his trip, not endure it! Now the physicist was not only a very polite man, but he was also shy and completely helpless when it came to combatting the will of a determined woman. Margaret stopped at his seat to point out the lovely valley below and give him a thorough review of the famous battle fought there during the War between the States. She named both generals commanding the contending forces, the number of dead and wounded on both sides. It was a good try, but it elicited only an appreciative nod and an absentminded smile.

Baffled, but undismayed, Margaret next brought a good-sized package of snapshots of her sister's husband's relatives in Prairie City and painstakingly explained all the complicated relationships as she slowly passed out the pictures. It should have won the day, but somehow it didn't, nor did the proposed game of Canasta which was politely declined.

The next time I saw our friend the physicist he told me the story and admitted that his lecture on that particular occasion had left something to be desired. "Someone should tell that nice girl that it never pays to work *too* hard to please," he concluded. Obviously I was elected to be that "someone." Margaret took my advice beautifully though momentarily I expected her to burst into tears. She had learned her lesson. However, I think, that added to the long list of questions put to a girl who aspires to stewardess service should be this one: "Are you sensitive to the unspoken desires and aversions of the people with whom you come in contact?" It is impossible to over-estimate the value of this rare characteristic.

If you are seriously thinking of taking up air service as a career, here is a suggestion which may help you over the first hurdle. If you've finished high school but have not gone to college, take a refresher course (at night school perhaps) in Rhetoric, English, Current Events, and Literature.

Almost eighty percent of our recruits hail from west of the Mississippi; sixty percent of them are blondes, thirty-six percent brunettes, and four percent redheads. It's a wonderful life, no matter from which side of the river you come or what the color of your hair.

Just to give you an idea of the diversified backgrounds of our United stewardesses: Jean Kerl, a former *Mainliner* stewardess out of Denver, did crypto-analytic research for the Army Signal Corps;

Betty Cooper of New York owned a beauty shop; Mary Jo Jones, also flying from New York, was head teller in an Ohio bank; and Marion Hartwick of Denver took to the air after several years with the State Department in such romantic sounding places as Algiers and Baghdad. Having tried flying, they all became loyal champions of the airways.

One of the very nicest features about the stewardess's job is the simple schedule by which she works. There are no irritating uncertainties—aside from the weather—no arbitrary changes in the carefully planned routine. On the first of each month every stewardess is given a printed schedule of flights for the month ahead, each girl scheduled for eighty-five hours of duty. Thus she knows exactly which days she will be on duty and which off and where she will be flying during that month. As to her duties, they certainly are not arduous. She will make out reports and check records; she will chat with passengers and point out places of interest (but remember, only if they seem interested); she will help passengers with plane and rail connections. She will serve meals and other refreshments; she will provide reading and writing materials, arrange pillows and blankets. She will give extra help to elderly passengers and mothers with young children, and to any other passengers who might require special attention.

Trips vary. One, for instance, may be from

Chicago to New York and return, another from Chicago to Los Angeles or San Francisco. The length of the trip naturally decides the length of the "lay over" at the away-from-home base. One definite rule is that a stewardess must have two hours off for every hour spent in the air, so on the Chicago to New York trip, though the stewardess *could* take a six-hour "off" period and still return the same night, the chances are she would not unless her schedule required it. She probably would stay the night at a hotel where the company maintains and pays for rooms for its stewardesses. In New York it is the St. Moritz; in Chicago the Congress; in Washington the Hay-Adams, opposite the White House; in Boston the Sheraton Plaza; in Denver the Cosmopolitan; in Salt Lake City the Utah; in San Francisco the Ben Franklin (at San Mateo); and in Seattle the Olympic. Meals, and transportation to and from the airport, are taken care of by the company.

The time-off period after a round trip flight usually amounts to from thirty-six to forty-eight hours at the stewardess's home base. She may spend it at home if her home is reasonably near the airport, or she may spend it at the Stewardess's Lounge. One of these delightful lounges is to be found at practically every major airport and they play a tremendous part in maintaining the universally high morale of

Interior of the stewardess lounge at Chicago Midway Airport

the young women who use them. Here there are showers, dressing rooms, rooms in which to do ironing or pressing or mending; here are comfortable sleeping quarters—two beds to a room—with radio, air conditioning, and a buzzer system. In addition there is a spacious sitting room with TV, cards and card tables, magazines, public and inter-com telephones. A matron looks after the rooms, and beds are made from seven in the morning until midnight.

Wherever she is, the stewardess is well cared for. Sometimes two, four, or even six girls will join forces in renting an apartment which becomes their home base. They enjoy living this way because it means they have a really good apartment which still is not expensive since several are contributing toward the rent. Also it gives the girls an opportunity to relax and visit away from work; to shop for bargain dresses and have a place in which to alter them, if need be, and compare notes; to entertain in the atmosphere of a home which is every girl's delight.

Salary is, naturally, of primary importance to all of us. It varies slightly within each company and may fluctuate with the passing years. At United Air Lines the starting salary is $290 a month and can go to $329 for the Hawaii run. The maximum, covering 85 hours per month, is $375 on the mainland and $426 for Hawaiian schedules. Stewardesses are eligible for pensions, health insurance, sick leave, and other benefits.

United Air Lines gives its accepted applicants free transportation to Cheyenne where they attend school eight hours a day, five days a week, for five weeks. The company provides meals, lodging, and a dollar a day for pocket money. There is no tuition fee. Meal service and other duties are practiced in realistic mockups of *Mainliner* cabins.

Qualified applicants must be single, at least five feet two inches tall, but not over five feet eight inches. Their weight should be one hundred and thirty-eight pounds or less in proportion to height. They must be at least twenty years old but not yet twenty-seven. The stewardess may work as long as she maintains her health, her figure, her general good looks and high spirits.

United Air Lines' 1959 "peige" uniform

About uniforms. The newest, and I think the prettiest uniform we have had, came in about 1959. It is in a new color, *peige*, which is beige with a slightly pink overtone, really awfully smart. With it we wear dark blue shoes and bag and a small hat of *peige*. We used to pay for our own uniforms, but today the company pays one half and bears the cost of all dry cleaning.

Speaking of uniforms, I must digress for a mo-

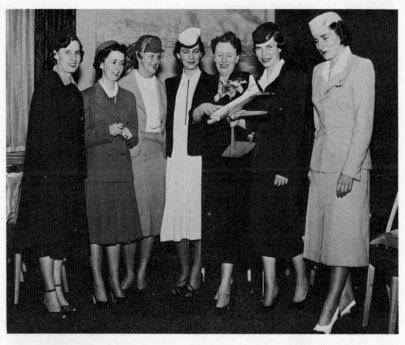

Mary O'Connor's 20th anniversary party. Uniforms from left to right: 1930, 1933, 1937, 1939, 1951 winter and summer.

Miss O'Connor with her honorary diploma, presented in 1956, but predated May 1933.

STEWARDESS DIPLOMA

THIS IS TO CERTIFY THAT

MARY E. O'CONNOR

has satisfactorily completed the prescribed training course for the

MAINLINER STEWARDESS

and is hereby qualified and commissioned to perform the duties

pertaining thereto for UNITED AIR LINES

Awarded this 18th day of May, 1933

W. A. Patterson
President

H. F. Barnes
Superintendent Flight Service

ment to tell you of a memorable occasion—my twentieth anniversary with United Air Lines. There was a celebration in Boston, and the stewardesses dressed in the old uniforms that were worn in "my day"—from 1930 to 1951.

These days, graduation exercises are held, and diplomas are awarded. I never received a diploma. One day, in November 1956, I said jokingly to Tom Dawson, Superintendent of Stewardess Service, that I was flying as a stewardess without benefit of diploma. He said nothing at the time, but a few months later he invited me to the graduation luncheon in Denver. Much to my surprise and delight, I was presented with a diploma at that luncheon.

chapter 7

THE *Mainliner* stewardesses never have thought of their part in the field of aeronautics as a job. To them it has always been rather a delightful way of life, almost a vocation, if you will, and they are all reluctant, when circumstances require it, to relinquish old ties, old associations.

In 1941, with something of the sort in mind, Mrs. Leonard Ceasar of Chicago, the former Jackie Jos, organized a club for United Air Lines ex-stewardesses. Only United ex-stewardesses were eligible to join. The meetings, held once a month, were simply social get-togethers, luncheons, or matinee parties. However, these girls soon realized that any organization, whose sole premise is a few hours of chatter about old times, can easily wear itself thin. They knew there should be some serious purpose behind their meetings; some charitable cause should benefit. They put it to a vote and the first organization to benefit was the Florence Crittenden Anchorage in Chicago. We hear great things from the eleven branches scattered across the country. Former "sky girls," most of them busy wives and mothers now, are giving time and energy, helping in varied capacities in whatever work the United Air Lines alumnae is doing in their city.

In 1950, twenty years of stewardess service were celebrated. There were parties in many of the large cities, but I had the luck to attend the one in Denver at which the real pioneers—Ellen Church and Stephen Stimpson—were present.

When you are happy in your work you do not realize how time is flying—one of life's dullest truisms, certainly—until suddenly you begin to hear by the grapevine that a celebration in your honor is afoot. You don't know exactly why, but this comes as a funny little shock. Celebration? For you? But what for? Ah, yes, then you remember that misty morning back in 1933 when butterflies fluttered in your stomach and everything in you seemed to slide a little drunkenly off balance as you were borne aloft on your first ride in an airplane.

But was that, *could* that have been so long ago? It was. You had to admit you'd been flying for twenty-five years. Now your company and the lads

Miss O'Connor cuts the cake at the party in Denver celebrating the 20th anniversary of stewardess service. Next to her, Ellen Church; then, Stephen Stimpson, Margaret Arnott, another of the original stewardesses, and Janet Winkler, the 3,000th

and gals who had been part of those years wanted to say in some fashion, "Hi, Mary! Nice going!" Somehow, my collar was suddenly too tight, my chest felt as though it just might explode, and my eyes couldn't read even the large print. Believe it or not, there was to be a party, and what a party it was!

First of all, the celebration itself was made up of so many lovely tributes of various sorts—seven hundred and fifty of them—that even today I remember the special thrill that came with the opening of them throughout that happy day. Letters, telegrams, poems, gifts, these came in an endless stream, among them Arthur Godfrey's twenty-five long-stemmed red roses with a note which read, "Dear Mary, just want to be among your many friends honoring you tonight. Congratulations and God bless you. Arthur Godfrey." Stewardesses from Capital Air Lines sent special greetings, a sweet gesture, I thought, coming from a rival line; and our

Arthur Godfrey

own stewardesses, one from each station, sent a tiny airplane painted with United's colors and my name on it.

On the anniversary day itself I left on a chartered flight to Madison, Wisconsin with President (then Senator) John Kennedy. In Madison four of United's pilots who are "the Minute Men" of the Air National Guard, were putting on a beautiful show with jets, maneuvers in formation for some special occasion, and had there been time, Captain Ed Mack Miller, the leader, had suggested taking me up for my first Jet flight. However, we had to curtail our celebration and the four "Minute Men" and Frank Cole, one of our salesmen, and I had a festive dinner instead at the Edgewater Hotel in Madison. The following evening those same nice lads took me to dinner at Mader's, in Milwaukee, had a gorgeous "Anniversary" cake, and had the orchestra play the "Anniversary Waltz." To sophisticates that may sound corny; to me it was beautiful.

Back in Chicago, the girls in my office gave a quiet, intimate little dinner in my favorite Hawaiian restaurant. Then Mr. Patterson had the staff members and the girls down to the Executive Dining Room for coffee and presented me with a certificate of membership to the Quarter-of-a-Century Club. With it came a handsome clock with perpetual mo-

tion, a barometer and weather vane, and, best of all, an inscription which I cherish.

We have a custom at United which I think is one of the most heartwarming in American industry. Every six months a very special party is given at one of the major cities on the route for all the employees whose twenty-fifth anniversary with the company came within those six months. Ours was in Seattle at the Olympic Hotel and I was the only "gal" among fifty pilots who had started when I did 'way back yonder.

What a glorious time we did have! There was a banquet, naturally, and there were boating trips, a

Miss O'Connor with other United Air Lines employees celebrating 25 years of service—Seattle, May 1958

trip to the magnificent Boeing Airplane plant, from British Overseas Airways a trip to London and other European points, and through it all the nostalgic echo of "Do-you-remember-when?" that kept us all constantly between shouts of laughter and a hint of tears.

And then it was all over. How do you thank people for so much affection and for showing it in so many eloquent ways? You just cannot to save your soul. You may accuse yourself of being a sentimental goose, but you know you will never, never forget and that to the end of your days you will thank a benevolent Deity for letting you share so many glorious years with those friends of the airways.

The day of the Executive Plane is over and the *Mainliner O'Connor* per se, like a faithful battleship past its first shining perfection, will be put into mothballs. The age of the Jet has dawned, a marvelous age in which to be just starting out on a flying career. I enjoyed every golden moment of mine, and I hope the girls today will find the thrill of growing up with a brand new industry every bit as satisfying as I did. More power to them and God bless them.

The new DC 8 Jet Mainliner cruises at up to 600 m.p.h.

Index

Index

Index

PRINTED IN U.S.A.